This is a book that clarifies what we all, at some level, know but don't do. Paul J. Meyer makes a persuasive case for forgiveness as a choice, not an emotion, something we do, not something we ought to do, and something from which we receive enormous benefits. Great stories and great lessons from a master teacher!

Bob Buford, Founder and Chairman, Leadership Network
Author of **Halftime** *and* **Finishing Well**

I have first-hand knowledge of half a dozen situations where Paul demonstrated a forgiving spirit. He still amazes me by his ability to take a punch … and then lend a hand. He is an amazing forgiver! Paul's writing style turns this easily misunderstood topic into a clear, step-by-step process to freedom through forgiveness. You are in for a treat!

John Edmund Haggai, Founder of the Haggai Institute

I've known Paul J. Meyer for 50 years. I was his pastor when he was 23 years old and have been his friend ever since. One of his Forgiveness in Action stories happened while I was his pastor. I've seen him forgive the seemingly unforgivable! If you—in any way, shape, or form—struggle with forgiveness, you need to read Paul's book.

Dr. W. M. "Bill" Hinson, first pastor and lifelong friend

Paul J. Meyer has been a mentor of mine for many years. In this book he teaches that forgiveness is not an emotion. It is a choice, one that each of us should choose to make. It changed his life and will change yours, too!

John C. Maxwell, **New York Times** *Best-Selling Author,*
Founder—INJOY Stewardship Services & EQUIP

I have become friends with the people who speared my father to death. In fact, they have become family. The men who killed my dad, Nate Saint, have become substitutes for him in my life. It's a God thing. I don't have a formula for it, but if God can do that in my life, He can do it in your life, too.

Steve Saint, speaker and author of **The Great Omission**

Nothing is more central to our well-being, spiritually, emotionally, and yes, physically, than our ability to give and receive forgiveness. Paul J. Meyer has given us an IMAX picture of what forgiveness looks like. His real-life stories illustrate, demonstrate, and motivate us to experience and practice forgiveness. Having been Paul's pastor for the last 25 years, I have had the joy of seeing him live out this beautiful ministry of forgiveness in his personal and professional life. This book is more than a "must read"—it is part of our personal health regimen.

D. Michael Toby, Pastor of First Woodway Baptist Church

Forgiveness has an uncanny way of bringing incredible good out of incredibly bad situations.

It's amazing — nothing less than a miracle.

Forgiveness

... The Ultimate Miracle

Paul J. Meyer

New York Times best-selling author

Foreword by Ken Blanchard, co-author of *The One-Minute Manager* and *Lead Like Jesus*

Bridge-Logos

Orlando, FL 32822 USA

Bridge-Logos
Orlando, FL 32822 USA

Forgiveness ... The Ultimate Miracle
by Paul J. Meyer

Printed in the United States of America.

Library of Congress Catalog Card Number: 2006932357
International Standard Book Number 0-88270-234-3

G163.316.N.m608.352100

Contents

Acknowledgments

I would like to thank the many who contributed to this book, especially those who sent in real-life stories of hurt, pain, and forgiveness. What people go through on a daily basis is heart wrenching. Thank God for forgiveness!

Thanks also to my staff who helped gather these great stories and critique and edit the chapters of this book: Brian Mast, Linda Peterson, and Karon Freeman.

This book was not written from a research point of view, an academic point of view, or a theological point of view. It was written from a practical and personal point of view. I asked counselors, friends, pastors, employees, and acquaintances for real stories about forgiveness. You will be amazed by what you read!

The stories used in this book are true, though names, locations, and certain details have been changed to both protect the innocent and to clarify the points of the story. If we described your story in exact detail or used your name by accident, it was by no means intentional. It is our hope, however, that the stories strike close to home so that you will be challenged and encouraged to forgive.

Forgiveness really is the ultimate miracle!

Foreword

I am a big fan of Paul J. Meyer. He has *forgotten* more about motivation, leadership, and life than most of us have ever known. That's why I was thrilled when he sent me a copy of *Forgiveness ... The Ultimate Miracle* and asked if I would write a foreword for it.

As I sat down to read this manuscript, I was touched by every page and realized that everyone should read this book. Why? Because you'll never have real peace in life unless you learn to forgive not only others, but yourself.

Emmet Fox, in his classic interpretation of the Lord's Prayer, spent about twenty-five percent of his discussion on *"forgive us our trespasses as we forgive those who trespass against us."* He claims this clause is the turning point of the prayer and the strategic key to the whole New Testament. So, abundant life all starts with forgiveness.

As Paul says, "Forgiveness has an uncanny way of bringing incredible good out of incredibly bad situations." My mother always told me, "When people do something mean to you and you don't forgive them, it only hurts you. They could not care less."

I could go on and on about why I think forgiveness is so important, but I have a better idea. Act like a third-grade teacher when you read this book. Read it over, and over, and over again until you get it right, right, right. Let Paul J. Meyer be your forgiveness guide. Learn the benefits of forgiveness, learn to forgive others, yourself, and even God. And, best of all, learn to let forgiveness set you free.

Thanks, Paul, for sharing with us all about forgiveness. We will be indebted to you for a long time.

Ken Blanchard
Summer 2006

Introduction

As far as I can remember, my father ***never forgave a soul***. It didn't even matter if the "offending" individual was part of our family or not. Take Uncle Otto for example, my dad's only brother-in-law. Dad told him, "Stop speaking German in my house or you will never be permitted back inside these doors. We're in America now, so speak English."

Otto spoke German again, and that was that. No more Otto. He was never permitted in the home again. At Thanksgiving, Otto would park his car on the road at the end of the lane and his wife (my mom's sister) would walk 100 yards to our house and eat with us. Otto stayed in the car the entire time. I would sneak out the back door with a plate of food, hop the fence, scurry along the fence line until I was behind the car, and then climb back over the fence to give Otto his Thanksgiving meal.

My father had three sisters, but only one of them came to America. She lived just 40 miles from our home in California. At my birth, she had the misfortune of mentioning that I had large ears. From that moment on, my dad refused to talk to her. So, for 35 years, despite the fact that she lived close by and that she was my father's only relative in this country, he never spoke to her again!

No matter how hard or awkward it made life for him or our family, he refused to forgive anyone. As a child, I would be playing with a friend one day; then the next day my dad would tell me that I could never play with that boy again. Because Dad had a disagreement with the boy's father, I was not allowed to associate with my friend or any member of his family. Countless friendships were broken as a result of my dad's unwillingness to forgive.

Don't get me wrong. I love my dad. He was an absolute genius in many, many areas. I trace my determination to him, my constant quest for improvement definitely comes from his influence, and my industrious work ethic emanates from his example. He was a phenomenal teacher and example, and I thank God for him.

Without question, I would not be the man I am today if it were not for him, but he had a problem with forgiveness. He died agonizingly over a seven-year period, probably giving himself more than 5,000 shots of Demerol during those seven long years! I'm not a doctor, but I have a suspicion that much of what ailed him came as a result of his unforgiving attitude.

My mother, on the other hand, ***forgave absolutely everyone***. One evening when I was young, my mother had prepared a delicious dinner, working most of the day to get it just right. When my father came home, he was in a bad mood for some unknown reason and decided to take his frustration out at dinnertime. He took the four corners of the tablecloth, folding the entire meal of food and dishes up into a bundle, and threw it out the back door!

I couldn't believe my eyes! When I asked my mother why she didn't throw a skillet at him, she said, "I've been married to him for 20 years and have always turned the other cheek." Then she added, quoting from a Bible verse (Matthew 18:22) that meant a lot to her, "I have a long way to go until I reach 'seventy times seven.'" I could not believe my ears, but I never forgot what she said.

She could forgive because she wanted to forgive. She chose to forgive. She preferred to live with forgiveness than to live with unforgiveness. As a result, she had such peace and joy that it bubbled out of her life.

There I was, stuck between polar opposites. I loved both my parents and am still indebted to them for what they taught me, but in this area, I knew I had to ***choose*** forgiveness or ***reject*** it. Which was the better offer? When I was about 16 years old, I made a conscious decision to start forgiving people and to live a life of forgiveness. I had watched my parents and knew which of the two had more peace and joy. The difference was not hard to see.

"I like your deal better," I told my mom one day. **"You're happy and have lots of friends, but Dad's unforgiving and doesn't have as many."**

My mom explained, "Paul, you are at a crossroads. Your choice to forgive or not to forgive will impact the rest of your life."

She was exactly right. **So I chose forgiveness!**

CHAPTER ONE

The Benefits of Forgiving

Too many to count!

Forgiveness has an uncanny way of bringing incredible good out of incredibly bad situations. It's amazing—nothing less than a miracle. But people don't usually choose forgiveness until they come face to face with what they are missing. They want the benefits of forgiveness!

And when it comes to wanting the benefits of forgiveness, you certainly cannot blame them!

The two tenors

A history that perhaps few know of concerns two of the three world-renowned tenors who have delighted the world: Luciano Pavarotti, Placido Domingo, and José Carreras. People who have never been to Spain often know of the rivalry between the Catalans and the people from Madrid, as the Catalans have struggled for many years for autonomy in Madrid-dominated Spain.

Placido Domingo is from Madrid and José Carreras is from the Catalans. For political reasons, in 1984 they became artistic rivals and political enemies. Whenever an invitation would come from anyone in the world, both Placido Domingo and José Carreras stipulated in their contracts that they would accept the invitation only if the other one was not invited.

In 1987, at the height of his career, Carreras faced a much more implacable enemy than his rival, Placido Domingo. He was diagnosed with leukemia and was given a one-in-ten chance of survival. His fight against cancer was very consuming, and under these conditions, he could not work. In spite of having a reasonable fortune, the high cost involved in traveling once a month to the U.S. (Seattle) resulted in his weakened financial condition. After investing all his finances in treatments and bone marrow transplants, he was financially spent but yet had not recovered.

It was then that he discovered the existence of an organization in Madrid, the Hermosa Foundation, which was dedicated to helping leukemia patients. He applied, received assistance, and survived, thanks to the support of the Hermosa Foundation. Carreras won the battle and resumed his singing career.

Once again, José Carreras received the high compensation that an acclaimed vocal artist deserved, and in gratitude, he wanted to contribute back to the Hermosa Foundation. While reading the company statutes, he discovered that the Founder and President of the foundation was none other than Placido Domingo. José later found out that Domingo had created the foundation for one specific reason: to take care of Carreras. Domingo had remained anonymous so that Carreras would not feel humiliated for accepting help from his archrival.

Deeply touched, Carreras entered the stage at one of Domingo's concerts in Madrid, surprising Placido, and interrupted the event by humbly kneeling at Domingo's feet, thanking him publicly, and asking for his forgiveness. Placido helped him to stand up, and with a strong hug, they sealed the beginning of a great friendship.

In an interview with Placido Domingo, a journalist asked him why he had established the Hermosa Foundation to benefit his rival, the only artist who could truly be his competition. Domingo's reply was short and definitive: "Because the world cannot afford to lose a voice like that."

Forgiveness has its benefits

One of the greatest aspects of forgiveness is that it works both ways. It feels good going out, and it feels good coming in. The giver and the receiver both benefit from the same action.

But forgiveness cannot be forced. You can't be made to forgive. It is a choice that you alone will make. When you begin to understand the width, depth, height, and completeness of the benefits that can only come from forgiveness, the choice becomes a much easier one.

Benefit #1 — It brings freedom

Mindy was four and her sister Molly was eight when the verbal putdowns began. Mindy can remember her older sister continuously making fun of her, incessantly chipping away at her budding self-confidence. As they got older, Molly took to flat-out lying in an effort to stay ahead of the ever-competitive Mindy.

> *Forgiveness feels good going out, and it feels good coming in.*

Years later, after graduating from college, getting married, and starting a family, Mindy began to recognize the effects of her sister's verbal abuse. In her work, she battled feelings of inferiority. In her marriage, she had trouble working through issues. Mindy pretty much hated her older sister. She knew that the compounded hurts were like chains, holding her to her past, but she didn't know how to break free.

It wasn't until her children were born that she came to a revelation. *"I knew that I didn't want my kids to repeat what had happened to me,"* she explains. *"It hurt me too much to let them do the same to each other."*

It was time to get free. Mindy wasn't sure if she and Molly would ever have a friendship, but Mindy's focus was finding freedom so that she could move on. She chose to forgive Molly and release the hate that had been building for over 30 years. She felt free for the first time.

From there, she worked on her own attitudes and thought patterns to strengthen her self-image. All the while, she carefully monitored her children. "My goal is for them to be each other's best support team," she points out. "I want them to believe in each other. Sure, they will be interested in different things and have different abilities, but they will be each other's cheering team."

For Mindy, freedom meant forgiving her sister and cutting the chains that held her captive. It also meant rewriting her present so that her children would not grow up to repeat her past. Freedom immediately affected two generations!

Forgiveness brings freedom.

Benefit #2 — Forgiveness brings power

A wise mother once said, "The person who angers you, conquers you." Power is about being in control. Granted, there are things we cannot control in our lives, like rain and taxes, but when it comes down to the personal level, being in control is vitally important.

> *The price of forgiveness is always less than the price of unforgiveness.*

In the example of the two sisters, Mindy regained control by dealing with her resentment and forgiving her sister. The older sister, Molly, might not even be aware that her words had a devastating effect on her younger, impressionable sister, but that doesn't matter. The hurt was real and Mindy was held captive by unforgiveness.

Mindy gained her freedom by taking control. She took responsibility and decided what she would and would not do. It was then that she had power. That alone, is a good enough reason to extend forgiveness!

Forgiveness does not just happen. It is always an act of the will.

Benefit #3 — Forgiveness is good for your health

Those who have been hurt badly by someone and respond with, "*I would die before I forgive you!*" **usually do!** There are many bitter men and women who are intent on taking their hurts to their graves with them. Sadly, they often die prematurely from the effects of holding onto unforgiveness toward another person.

My dad is a prime example. He refused to forgive and took countless grudges and hurts with him to the grave. I have no doubt in my mind that his unforgiveness affected his health in a very negative way.

By forgiving, we remove the distance and walls that are between us.

We have all known people who remember a hurtful event like it was yesterday, although it happened 10, 20, or even 50 years ago! Why do they do that? Don't they know that it's affecting their health?

Some physicians call it "grudge-itis," but call it what you will, holding a grudge, reliving a hurt, or fostering hatred against someone is bad for your health. Studies show that people who forgive are healthier, have less stress, and have lower blood pressure. Those who refuse to forgive, on the other hand, have increased risk for heart disease, cardiovascular illness, and cancer. How's that for motivation!

Colin C. Tipping, who works with cancer patients to help them forgive, makes the following observation: **"Nearly all cancer patients, besides having a lifetime habit of suppressing and repressing emotions, are known to share a marked inability to forgive."**

The unforgiveness is literally eating them from the inside out! Some believe that over time an issue will go away, but forgetting, pretending, denying, or the act of trying to forget does not bring healing. Only forgiveness can bring healing. Author Lewis B. Smedes rightly states, "Forgive when you want to be healed."

Benefit #4 — Forgiveness releases your creativity

The story goes that, as Leonardo DaVinci was painting the famous Last Supper, he painted the face of his enemy as the face of Judas. Surely he enjoyed the fact that he was forever immortalizing his enemy in his art! What a sweet way to get revenge.

> *Forgiveness will release your creativity.*

But as he did so, something strange happened. He couldn't finish the picture of Christ. His creativity was stifled. He tried, but couldn't do it. It was as if he was wrestling in his mind. Suddenly he realized what he must do. He forgave his enemy and erased his enemy's face from the painting. That very night he finished the face of Christ.

Forgiveness released DaVinci's creativity, and forgiveness will release your creativity as well.

Author D. Patrick Miller notes, "To find your missing creativity, release a little of your attachment to the worst injury ever done to you." Good advice—because it works!

Benefit #5 — Forgiveness restores your relationship with God

Gene is a Christian man, a loving father, and a great businessman. The only problem is that he hasn't spoken to his brother in five years. Five years ago, within a period of a few months, both of their parents died.

"My brother handled their passing away and their funerals so poorly that I refused to talk to him," explained Gene. "His actions hurt me deeply. I was angry, hurt, and offended."

Not long ago, I explained to Gene that his unforgiveness was affecting his relationship with God. Having never considered that before, Gene thought about it, prayed about it, and came to realize that it was true.

So Gene chose to forgive, picked up the phone, and called his brother. "It was probably the best conversation we have had in 20 years," Gene exclaimed! "After our conversation, the sun shone a little brighter, the birds seemed to sing a little sweeter, and I felt more of a connection with God than ever!"

Then the amazing happened. The next day, Gene spent several hours with his brother! This was on Thursday. On Sunday, Gene's brother died of a heart attack. After the funeral, Gene drove to my house and told me, "Thank you for telling me to forgive. You were completely right. We forgave and it saved me from a lifetime of guilt. I hate to think what my life would have been like with the guilt of not having forgiven him."

Forgiveness separates us from other people just as it separates us from God, but by forgiving, we remove the distance and walls that are between us. Is unforgiveness ever worth losing or minimizing your relationship with God?

Never!

Benefit #6 — Forgiveness is easier than unforgiveness

The act of choosing to forgive is not easy at the moment of hurt and pain, but in the long run, it is the only way to go. The natural response may be to get mad, act hateful, and be unforgiving, but though these things come easily, ***they are NOT the easiest route.*** The easiest route is the route that brings the most benefits ***in the end***, and that route is always the path of forgiveness.

Charlie "Tremendous" Jones once said, "Our unwillingness to forgive when we've been deeply hurt breeds self-pity and bitterness."

Who wants to be bitter and wallow in self-pity? What a wasted life! Thankfully, the reverse also holds true. By forgiving, we are training ourselves to be strong, confident, joyful, peaceful, happy, and loving. These positive attributes end up affecting every part of our lives.

An attitude of forgiveness leads to a much easier life than an attitude of unforgiveness!

Benefit #7 — Forgiveness brings restoration (sometimes)

Forgiveness will sometimes bring about restoration, but not always. If someone is dead, for example, you can't do much about restoring that relationship. You can forgive and move on, but there will never be the joyful restoration that comes when offending parties come back together.

The lack of restoration by no means undermines your forgiveness. You might not feel a sense of "closure," but the forgiveness is just as valid.

Rosa's husband suffered a massive stroke and lay dying in the hospital. "I wish I could tell him how much I love him," she sobbed, looking at his frail body outlined by the bed sheets. The truth was that they weren't even sleeping in the same bed, and their long-standing 20-year feud was known around the county. She wanted closure, but the restoration she wanted was not possible.

> *"Hating someone and holding onto bitterness builds a prison around us. Forgiving others frees us." – Steve Saint*

She could, however, forgive her husband for his infidelities and release him. That she did. At the funeral, her tears were genuine. She had forgiven him. She just wouldn't get a chance at restoration.

My own sister is a great example here. She came to my house one Thanksgiving. She was in a lot of pain with neck spasms and other physical ailments. It was as if she had been in a car accident. Later that night, as we relaxed in the hot tub and talked about our childhood, I leaned toward her and said, "Do you mind if I give you a bit of advice?"

She nodded.

"Remember how Dad never forgave anyone? Remember how much of a hard time he gave you while you were dating? I think your neck spasm and your other ailments are a result of an unforgiving attitude toward Dad."

We prayed right there and asked God to soften her heart, to cleanse her, and to heal her. Within 24 hours, the tension left her neck.

She called me a month later and said, "The biggest weight is off my shoulders! I don't know why, but I'm happier, I'm more self-confident, I feel less judgmental, I like myself more, I feel in control, my health is improving, and other people are commenting about how happy I look!"

Though our father was dead and she couldn't restore her relationship with him, she could forgive him ... and immediately benefit from it.

Benefit #8 — Forgiveness brings hope, joy, and a brighter future

Tonya and Eddie were married almost 15 years when he served her divorce papers. She felt as if she had been hit by a truck! "I put up with his anger issues, his midnight shift at the hospital, and his extended vacations away with his buddies," she explained. "I take care of our two boys 24 hours a day, and then he has the audacity to tell the judge that I'm abusive and not a part of our children's lives!"

The two boys, ages six and four, desperately needed both a mommy and daddy at home; there was no question about that, but Eddie wouldn't go to counseling with her. She found out later that he had gone to their pastor and convinced the pastor that she was a deranged mother. To top it off, the pastor's daughter (also divorced) counseled Eddie herself, and things turned romantic.

Tonya needed to get out of the emotional and negative whirlwind around her. She moved into an apartment nearby and took action. She decorated her new place, got a pet, and found a job. She worked her schedule around picking up her boys, shuttling them to and from their dad's a few times a week, and learning to be a single mom.

Just six months later, Tonya pointed out, "It was an incredibly hard time initially, but the more I found myself and the more I forgave, the more hope and joy I discovered. The forgiving part is a process, but I want to be free from Eddie so badly. I want to look to the future and see good things, and I'm beginning to do that now."

Forgiveness provides hope, joy, and a bright future that nothing else can.

Benefit #9 — Forgiveness allows God to bring justice

Benjamin Franklin noted, "Doing an injury puts you below your enemy; revenging one makes you even with him; forgiving sets you above him." We all want justice. It is an innate desire within us, but we seldom have the power to bring about justice.

What's more, justice isn't only about a thief going to prison. The verbally abused child, the emotionally damaged spouse, and the maligned employee will never see *their* perpetrators behind bars. What they have lost, nobody will be held accountable for. What type of justice could ever satisfy?

This is where God steps in if we let Him. His desire is to bless us, remove our shame and disgrace, and replace it all with a *"double portion"* because he is the Lord who loves justice (Isaiah 61:7-8). He loves to bring good out of bad situations, and that is the type of justice that satisfies.

But before God can work on your behalf, you must release bitterness and forgive. This both helps you survive and thrive and allows God to work the amazing on your behalf.

What types of justice could ever satisfy?

Sally moved a lot due to her husband's work. She was fine with it, but it was her two sons who seemed to pay the biggest price. At school in one remote town, her sons were repeatedly teased, picked on, and occasionally beaten up. She went through every emotion during the years they lived there. She was mad at her husband for bringing them there, mad at herself for not being able to protect her children, and finally mad at God for allowing it to happen. When they moved away, she tried to forgive and release her bitterness, but didn't think she would ever see justice served.

Years later, after her boys were grown, had completed college, and were working in very successful careers, Sally returned to that same town for a friend's funeral. It didn't take long to realize how fortunate she really was. Few of the children who grew up with her boys ever left town, much less went to college. Most had minimum-wage jobs, lived in one-bedroom houses, "cursed like pirates," got married because they were pregnant or got a girl pregnant, and expected little else for their own children.

She admits, "I was shocked at the hopelessness. I could feel it in the air. And the belief in a better future was at absolute zero! I see how fortunate and blessed I really am. I felt sorry for them, even the boys who hurt my children."

It was then that she realized the justice of her situation. In fact, it was more than justice. She had a husband and a wonderful life herself, her boys had great jobs and incredible opportunities in front of them, and those who had tried to step on her children had less than nothing. Sally could see how God had worked on her behalf. She had so much to be thankful for.

> *Forgiveness is first a choice and then an action.*

Our job is to let go, to forgive, and to trust God to work on our behalf. He has it under control. The Bible says that He will never leave us and never forsake us, and though we don't know how long it will take for justice to come about, we can trust that He will bring it to pass.

When you let God bring the justice, it will be more than you could have asked or imagined!

Choose because of the benefits

Much more could be said about the benefits of forgiveness, but the point is this: **to forgive is to benefit!** If you want these and other benefits, then let nothing stand in your way. Forgiveness is first a choice and then an action.

Practically speaking, it makes no sense that people would rather have ulcers, heart attacks, emotional problems, mental problems, and more, than simply forgive those who have done them wrong.

Decide that you will never settle for anything less than the benefits that come from forgiveness!

Putting forgiveness to work in my own life

Many years ago, I was encouraged to move to Texas and work for a national marketing company. I helped pull them from bankruptcy and increased their sales by 1500% in a 24-month period.

The evening after a convention celebrating our greatest year, I was called to meet with the board of directors. On the way to the meeting, I thought to myself, *"I don't need any rewards, titles, or positions. I am happy doing what I'm doing, helping build the company and making money through commissions."*

When I walked into the meeting, I knew that all was not well. The board told me point blank, "You are making too much money."

My response was, "I don't make the rules. I just play by them." Though my income from my commissions was more than the income of the top three board members combined, it didn't logically make sense that it would bother them.

I added, "I'm sorry I sold so much. Would you have preferred that I sold less?"

Because I made more money than they did, playing by their own rules, they fired me. (I later checked with another company and found out that my commissions were half of what they should have been!)

I went home and thought about it and prayed about it. I knew in my heart that if God closed one door, then He would open another. I chose to forgive and get on with my life. My plan had been to start my dream company, Success Motivation® Institute, Inc. (SMI) the next year, so I just moved up my timetable and started right away.

The rest, as they say, is history. I've made more money with my own companies than I could have ever made working for this national marketing company. And by the way, I've never fired someone for making too much money!

CHAPTER TWO

What Forgiveness Is and Is NOT

This will set you free!

Forgiveness must begin with a hurt; otherwise there is nothing to forgive. Unfortunately, there seems to be no limit to the hurt people will inflict on each other. Here is one incredibly brave woman's story.

Raped and abused in her own home

On a September night in 2002, I was brutally, sexually assaulted at knifepoint. It happened in my home while I was alone. I endured four hours of being bound and subjected to continuous abuse. I was stripped of all personal dignity and security. To top it off, this perpetrator threatened to commit suicide in front of me as "punishment" for what he had done.

I wanted him to do it, to end his life at this point. Not only was I afraid for my life, but for the life of my family. Somehow, I was able to talk him out of it and out of what he was doing to me. He left the house.

Nine days later, this individual found his way once again into my home and proceeded to inflict upon me another four hours of the same treatment. This time, however, it was more vicious because he already knew what physically hurt me the most.

Again, he talked about killing himself, but he had decided that I would lead the way. He began by hacking at his forearm with a butcher knife. At the sight of blood flowing from his arm, I started to pray. I thought I was going to die, but I was not afraid. I knew that I was safe in God's hands. I was afraid of what my family would have to endure after finding two bloody corpses in the house.

Amazingly, again I was able to talk him out of what he was doing. I actually drove him to the hospital. In the emergency room, he confessed to a nurse, who in turn called the police. He was arrested that night and has not known freedom since.

This man pled guilty to six counts of aggravated sexual assault and is currently serving a fifteen-year sentence. This man was my husband.

I went to visit him while he was in the county jail prior to sentencing. With much fear and emotion, I looked him in the eyes and I told him that I forgave him for what he had done to me.

He cried. I don't know if it was relief or remorse. Strangely, I was tempted to drop the charges in an effort to get him out of jail, but I stood my ground and was present at his sentencing.

Members of his immediate family shunned me because they felt that I hadn't really forgiven him since I "allowed" him to go to prison after all. I explained that I forgave him for three reasons:

#1 – Because he was my husband. I would not believe that the man whom I loved and married was the same man that had attacked me. It had to be some psychotic break with reality.

#2 – I knew that it would help me immensely during the healing process. I did not want to be consumed by rage or hate.

#3 – Last, and most importantly, Jesus forgave us all. Who am I to withhold forgiveness or pass judgment?

That I forgave him did not diminish the fact that he needed to pay the consequences for his actions. His family couldn't understand this.

Forgiving him helped me in many ways. It gave me an immediate sense of peace and clarity that enabled me to continue my daily "life" (i.e. going to work, paying the bills, etc.).

Forgiving my husband also allowed me to do much-needed self-analysis and emotional work. I came to believe that God gave me a second chance. He showed me the way out of my previously erroneous lifestyle and put me back on the right path. I firmly believe that it is because of God's grace and no other reason that I live and breathe today.

Since that time, I have purposefully changed my life. I moved to a new city and am currently following my dream of becoming a registered nurse. In retrospect (this might sound crazy to some people), I am content with the fact that what happened to me happened. Forgiveness gave me a new life. I have gained back what I lost that week and much more. I gained a new relationship with myself, my family, my neighbors, and most importantly with God. I never want to go through anything like that again and wish nobody else would either. But, as I sit here today, I would endure it all over again to get the same results. I may even categorize this as one of the best things that has happened to me.

Unraveling the confusion around forgiveness

People have very different definitions of forgiveness. Not to mention the added complexities of different denominations, cultures, religions, viewpoints, hurts, and experiences. Forgiveness is simply misunderstood.

Author Lewis B. Smedes wisely notes, "Often, people who don't forgive don't understand what forgiveness is." But leaving forgiveness undefined will not help you deal with life. It won't provide you with the answers that you need. Only forgiveness offers the benefits of forgiveness.

> *Forgiveness is not signing up to be a sucker.*

Part of the additional challenge is this: **Your definition of forgiveness will determine how you will use it.** If forgiveness means to pardon, and you have no intention of pardoning, then forgiveness is not an option for you. If forgiveness is forgetting, and you can't forget, then you won't forgive. It's as simple as that.

Understanding what forgiveness is and is NOT is an absolute must!

What forgiveness is:

Can you define forgiveness, given all the complexities and differences out there? Yes, you can, but the truth is, **you *need* to define forgiveness**. Only when you can define it can you do it. Did you catch that? Only when you define forgiveness can you actually forgive someone.

Forgiveness is: acknowledging the hurt

The fact that you were hurt is where forgiveness begins. It must begin there. Denying that you were hurt will undermine everything. It all begins with accepting that you were hurt.

Forgiveness is: keeping your eyes open

You are aware of the hurt, yet you are still willing to forgive. You see the pain for what it is, you know who did it, and you are honest with yourself. Your eyes are wide open. No pretending or playing games. And with what you see, you are willing to forgive and move on.

Forgiveness is: showing mercy

Mercy is the last thing that people who hurt you expect to receive. But if you have chosen to forgive, then mercy should be what they see and hear. Retaliation is what they deserve, but mercy is the fruit of forgiveness.

Forgiveness is: keeping no record of wrongs

Though you might not forget a hurt for a very long time after you've extended forgiveness, to forgive is to purposefully keep no record of wrongs. It's like you bury the list and choose not to dig it up. A spouse or neighbor who is quick to bring up past failures has not forgiven at all.

Forgiveness is: living free from bitterness

People who can remember the very day and the hour that they were hurt are usually full of bitterness. They literally "live" back in that moment, even if it was 50 years ago! To forgive is to release the bitterness. Do you want to poison your own life because of what someone else did? Forgiveness is living free from bitterness.

> *Retaliation is what they deserve, but mercy is the fruit of forgiveness.*

Forgiveness is: taking responsibility

The people you forgive are the ones responsible for the hurt they caused you. You are not responsible for their actions. Let them take their responsibility and you take yours. You are responsible for your own life, so choose the freedom, peace, and hope that you want. That is taking responsibility.

Forgiveness is: being honest about reality

To forgive is to honestly evaluate your situation and your options. You might be reconciled with the person who hurt you ... and you might not. Sometimes it's possible and sometimes it isn't because it always takes two people for a relationship to be restored. Begin with forgiveness, and then be honest about reality. If restoration occurs, great, but if not, you have already forgiven.

Forgiveness is: an attitude

Forgiveness really begins with a choice you make. This choice permeates your mind to the point where it is reflected in your attitude. You think forgiveness and you act forgiveness. It comes out of you because it's what you see, it's what you think, and it's what you believe.

Forgiveness is: a lifestyle

When forgiveness becomes a habit, it has become a lifestyle. This is a wonderful place to be. You don't have to weigh each situation and consciously decide if you are going to forgive this time or not.

Instead, you move from hurt to healing because it's what you do. It's how you choose to live your life.

What forgiveness is NOT

The most confusing part about forgiveness is what we have learned from others. Nine times out of ten, **what we have seen, experienced, or been told, is not forgiveness at all**. Bad definitions of forgiveness will do you more harm than good.

Forgiveness is not: approval

Never is forgiveness a simple act of approval. That is nothing less than denial, blindness, ignorance, and stupidity. To approve is to willfully accept. If you don't want your hurt to be repeated — on you or on others — then do NOT approve of it! Approval is acceptance. Forgiveness is not.

Forgiveness is not: forgetting

Those who forgive usually forget over time, but purposefully forgetting a hurt is little more than suppressing your emotions. Author D. Patrick Miller states, "Trying to forget is just another means of denial." This, as you know, is no way to go about living life. Sooner or later, what you've been suppressing for years will come back to haunt you. The sexually abused daughter who grew up, forgave her dad, purposefully forgot what he had done, and then left her own daughter in his care ... was regrettably, sadly, and insanely allowing the past to repeat itself.

> *Forgiveness is not pretending something never happened.*

Forgiveness is not: justifying

Sure, there are a million possible reasons why people might have hurt you, but that does nothing to lessen the hurt they caused you. Knowing what happened is a fact. It might help you understand people and their actions, but facts are not forgiveness. Always get the facts, but never allow facts to justify someone's actions.

Forgiveness is not: an obligation

Nobody can force you to forgive. Forgiveness is always a choice. Yes, it is highly recommended, good for your health, etc., but it always starts with you making a conscious decision to forgive, after you've worked through the hurt and pain. If you "forgive" out of obligation, then there is no reason to work through an issue, to be honest, or to think. To forgive out of obligation is not forgiveness at all.

Forgiveness is not: giving in

Those who have been hurt often find themselves in similar, if not exactly the same, situations. It happened once and it will happen again if you allow it to. Forgiveness is not giving in. You have the right to refuse further hurt, pain, and abuse. If you give in, you are excusing, pardoning, and accepting more of the same. You do not need to stay with people who hurt you. The end result of allowing greater hurt will never produce anything good.

Forgiveness is not: reconciliation (restoration)

If reconciliation comes after you forgive, then great, but it is not a prerequisite for forgiveness. Always remember that forgiveness comes before reconciliation. It takes two willing people to make reconciliation possible. The son who forgives his dead father can experience the benefits of forgiveness, but the father-son relationship cannot be reconciled or restored. Forgiveness is complete by itself. Reconciliation is awesome, but it's entirely separate from forgiveness.

> *To forgive is to use your heart and your head.*

Forgiveness is not: re-hiring

Just as you are under no obligation to forgive, so you are under no obligation to re-hire the person who hurt you or someone you know. With the abusive boyfriend, the questionable babysitter, and the cheating employee, you have to use your head. Get wise counsel from others, but there are certain situations that you should never repeat. To forgive is to use your heart ***and*** your head.

Forgiveness is not: trust

Forgiveness shows love, strength, and kindness. It means you have honestly come to terms with both the person and what was done to you. But forgiveness does not mean that you trust the person as you did before. To do so would be naïve. Trust that is destroyed must be rebuilt, brick by brick. In time, the individual might earn your trust, but it must be earned. Forgiveness has little to do with trust.

Forgiveness is not: getting even

Try as you might, you will never get even with someone who hurt you. That is because we all have different scales. Some think that they will feel complete or whole when there is justice, but forgiveness is not based on outside circumstances. All the justice in the world cannot make you forgive. It always begins as an internal choice. Getting even is the impossible dream of those who will not forgive.

> *Forgiveness is giving up your right to hurt someone.*

Forgiveness has its price

Forgiveness is neither cheap nor easy. It takes time and effort. It has its price, with the biggest price of forgiveness being determined by you and your situation. Most see it as a "little thing" to forgive the bully from 4th grade as compared to a rapist, murderer, spouse abuser, or thief, but regardless, there is a price for forgiveness.

For many, **the price is giving up their right to get even**. For others, it is letting go of painful, yet familiar memories. For some, the price of forgiveness is starting over from scratch in a new city with a new job. Everyone and every situation is unique, thus making the price of forgiveness unique and personally costly.

Consider Mike, for example. When his only son was accidentally killed in a drive-by shooting, Mike vowed he would never forgive the killer. "The future was unlimited and bright for my son," Mike laments, "Now, I feel like I've lost everything!"

People experience unimaginable pain, hurt, and abuse, but these are not a measurement of the price of forgiveness. No, the price of forgiveness is not measured by the hurt that is caused. **The real price of forgiveness is what it costs you to give up an unforgiving attitude.**

Did you catch that? The price of forgiveness is what it costs you to give up an unforgiving attitude. Are you willing to pay that price? Are you willing to forgive?

Choosing not to forgive has too great a price tag.

Mike figured this out for himself: "A year after the accident, my son's killer was convicted and sent to jail, but I was still a mess. It was then that I realized that justice was not going to heal my hurts, anger, resentment, and loss. I wanted my life back."

Of course, there was nothing that Mike could do to bring his son back, but he could do something to get his own life back—forgive. Choosing not to forgive has too great a price tag.

Is it worth holding onto something that happened in the past? By not forgiving, you are not hurting the person who hurt you ... **you are only hurting yourself.** The price of forgiveness is small in comparison to the price of unforgiveness.

If, on the other hand, you are the one asking for forgiveness from someone for something you have done, there is a rightful price tag affixed to forgiveness. It's called "restitution."

Suppose you broke your neighbor's window with a baseball. You are asking to get away with it ***unless*** you offer to pay for it. Restitution costs something. Usually it's money, but it can be a lot of things, depending on what you've done. If you are the one asking for forgiveness, you must make it right or at least offer to do so. If you don't, you are not asking for forgiveness.

The neighbor is free to say, *"Don't worry about it"* or *"Okay, I'll send you the bill."* Either way, you have taken responsibility for your actions and done an honest job seeking forgiveness.

The need for forgiveness only increases

Inevitably, someone is going to hurt us. The longer we are alive, the greater our chances of getting hurt. It's just a fact of life. Howard Olsen points out, "Life without suffering is impossible, and anyone who lives running from pain lives no life at all."

The need to forgive will only increase over time. There isn't much you can do about that. And no matter how absurd the action against you or how badly you hurt, forgiveness carries less of a price tag than unforgiveness.

Choosing to forgive brings sanity where insanity reigns, love where there are feelings of hate, and peace where there could be war. Although the opportunity for forgiveness only increases, so does your knowledge and ability to forgive.

Putting forgiveness to work in my own life

Bert overcharged me for construction supplies to the tune of about $15,000. When I found out, I drove straight to the job site and confronted Bert.

"Where is the $15,000 I advanced for this project?"

"I don't know," he replied.

"What do you mean you don't know? How could $15,000 just disappear? What's going on?"

I knew Bert was cornered. He was caught red-handed. Telling the truth seemed like his only option. "Okay, I've got a drug problem," he blurted out, beginning to cry uncontrollably. "I'm sorry. I needed the money and didn't know what else to do."

I could have fired Bert on the spot for swindling me out of $15,000. Adding in some jail time might also have helped. Instead, I looked Bert in the eye and said, "You have worked for me for 12 years. You are my friend and I forgive you. I'll help you lick this problem. The first thing we'll do is get you into drug rehab."

Bert could go to rehab, paid for by me, and still draw a check while he was gone. I knew I was being more than gracious, but I felt it was the right thing to do. "And when you get back," I added, "we'll work out a way for you to start paying me back, little by little."

What was Bert's response to this incredible second chance? He didn't take it. Perhaps it was a pride issue, not wanting to admit that he had a problem. Or maybe he was reluctant to go to rehab. Maybe it was the shame of getting caught. Whatever the case, he packed his bags and left the country, finding a construction job on a Caribbean island.

Looking back, I am still glad I offered him another chance, but I'm no pushover. I'll forgive instantly, but the other person has to meet me halfway if we are going to continue to work together. Forgiveness is not signing up to be a sucker.

CHAPTER THREE

10 Practical Steps to Forgiveness

Step by step, you can do this!

Forgiveness can be very practical at times. It makes sense. There are steps to take. It is logical ... until the hurt strikes close to home and the issue becomes personal! Emotions rage and tempers flare! The steps to forgiveness still apply, but in the thick of things, when you are raw and hurting, it may seem like there is no logic involved.

Barry and Martha Camp have experienced this firsthand. Here is their story.

Killed by a drunk driver

My wife and two children were driving back from the movie theater around 7:30 one September evening and were about a mile away from home when a drunk driver pulled right in front of them. It was a head-on collision. The two vehicles smashed together and slid off the road.

It happened so fast that my wife didn't even see it coming. Bam! Martha awoke to a man banging on her car door. "Tell me, is this a dream or is this real?" was the first thing she said.

"It's real!" he replied.

Martha was bleeding internally as well as from a gash on her forehead. Our daughter, Carrie, six years old, was wedged against the front windshield with an obvious broken arm. Our son, Mark, age nine, had been thrown forward and knocked unconscious.

I was at home mowing the lawn and didn't hear the phone ring. When I got inside, someone from our church called and told me that there had been an accident.

As a pastor, I am supposed to have the answers, but I drove to the hospital in a daze, praying and quoting Psalm 23 the whole way. I knew in my heart that it was serious. When I walked into the emergency room, the doctor gave me the horrible news: "I don't think your daughter is going to make it. We are putting her on life support for 48 hours to see if she'll make it, but it doesn't look hopeful."

I spent most of the night in the hospital, then went home to sleep a bit and gather some things. My brother flew in from Washington, D.C., and he and I drove back to the hospital. Martha was out of intensive care, but with the tubes down her throat, she could not talk. She gestured, "How are the children?"

Lying, I told her that they were okay.

In reality, Carrie was cold to the touch, and when they unplugged the life support system after 48 hours, she died. Mark was still unconscious, suffering from a severe concussion. His left side was paralyzed.

As I sat in the waiting room, my brother brought a man into the room. "Barry, this man has something to say to you."

The man was the drunk driver! He fumbled and stumbled with his words, trying to say he was sorry, knowing full well that there was nothing he could do to right the situation.

The more we talked, the more it became evident that he was a very messed up individual. I learned that he was driving without a license because it had been suspended for a previous DUI.

I looked him in the eye and said, "Look, I forgive you for what you did out of negligence and irresponsibility, but I have to ask you, are you happy with your life?"

He cried, "No. I want my life changed."

Right there in the waiting room, I prayed with the man who had killed my daughter. He asked God to forgive him and prayed that God would change his life. I marveled at this divine opportunity. I never saw the man again until he appeared in court for his sentencing.

To say the least, it was a horrendous time. We miss Carrie incredibly, but good has come of it. God is always able to make good come from horrible situations. While in surgery, the doctors discovered that Martha's intestines were in the wrong place, the result of an unknown birth defect. They were able to fix that, which no doubt saved her life down the road. Mark, who was paralyzed on his left side for an entire month, miraculously recovered completely.

Looking back, I've found that forgiveness is a large part of healing. Until you get to the point where you can release someone and forgive, the healing cannot start.

Forgiveness takes guts ... and brains!

Some people think that forgiveness is for the weak, the stupid, the cowardly, and the spineless. **Nothing could be further from the truth!**

Forgiveness requires guts, determination, perseverance, courage, and love. Dr. Fred Luskin says, "Forgiveness is an act that shows strength." It will test your metal, but when your burning desire is to forgive at all costs, you will follow through.

Forgiveness is also logical. It requires that you think about your present circumstances, make careful decisions, and plan for your future. It takes brains to forgive.

Forgiveness is also logical.

In addition, forgiveness is a much better option than unforgiveness. Common sense would tell you that freedom is better than prison, joy is better than hate, and life is better than death.

It's the people who prefer their lives of unforgiveness who are gutless and brainless. By pursuing forgiveness, you are taking the high road. You are rising up. You are becoming great. You are the one in charge.

Keep going! Don't let what anyone says slow you down in the slightest.

Learning how to forgive

Forgiveness really is something you learn to do. You get better at it the more you practice it. Like a sport or an instrument, the more you practice, the better you will be. Dr. Robert D. Enright explains, "Forgiveness is a skill. The more you forgive, the easier it gets."

It would be nice if forgiveness came naturally to us, but the reverse is typically true. We want to lash out, to settle the score, and we want it done yesterday! Unforgiveness is our usual "automatic response" when we are hurt.

Let's face it; living life opens you to hurt!

The truth is, most people just don't know how to forgive. They are caught between misconceptions about forgiveness and the strong natural desire to see the offending person pay. What do they do? Not much, and by default, they choose a semi-passive bitterness that pretends to be "over it" in public, but revels in the ongoing hurt in private.

Not quite a split personality, but certainly a confused one! There is no peace, joy, or freedom to be found. What they need is to learn how to forgive.

10 steps to forgiveness

If you are alive, you have experienced the need to forgive. Having friends opens you to hurt. Being married opens you to hurt. Pastoring a church opens you to hurt. Being part of a family opens you to hurt. Playing on a team opens you to hurt. Working a job opens you to hurt.

Let's face it; living life opens you to hurt! And there really isn't much you can do about it.

Can you stop the wind? No, but you can make a windmill. Can you stop the waves? No, but you can control the set of the sail. Can you stop getting hurt? No, but you can learn how to forgive.

If you don't, you will miss the opportunity in the wind, you will flounder in the ocean, and you will be held captive by unforgiveness.

To forgive and to move beyond the hurt, follow these proven steps:

Step #1 — Decide on the hurt

You've been hurt. You've been wronged. What happened? Who did it? What are all the details?

Regardless of the situation, **it must have happened to *you***, not your neighbor down the street or your people 100 years ago. It must be *your* hurt and *your* pain that you can attach a date and a time to.

Granted, sometimes a hurt might come through someone else, such as your child (maybe a bully hurt your son at school), a sibling (perhaps a nasty divorce devastated your sister), your spouse (maybe your husband was wrongly fired), or your parents (perhaps a crook CEO sank the business and lost your parents' life savings), but 99% of the time the hurt is a personal hurt.

And if it's your hurt, then you are the one who needs to deal with it. You can't brush it under the proverbial carpet as if it never happened. Denial has no place when it comes to deciding on the hurt. You simply need to state the facts. Spill the beans. Tell the whole truth. Put all the cards on the table.

Depending on your situation, you may choose to write it down or to work it through by talking to yourself. Either way, you must be clear in what happened and in how you were hurt. Decide on your hurt and make it plain.

Step #2 — Be real, be honest

How badly were you hurt? Do you need to scream at the top of your lungs? Don't be fake. Be honest. The pain is real. That is a fact.

Don't minimize your hurt. Denial is hard to fix at a later date. Let yourself grieve and cry if you need to.

Once you have acknowledged how you were hurt, it's time to be equally as honest and hold the offender accountable for his or her actions. You might not be able to send the individual to jail in your own power, but you can define that person as "guilty" in your own heart and mind. You have that power. And it is important that you use it.

> *Let yourself grieve and cry if you need to.*

Being real and honest is extremely important for your mental and emotional stability because you are being truthful about how you feel and about who did what. You are painting a clear picture, which you must have as you move forward. That is because **it is impossible to get past a hurt that you cannot define.**

Being real and honest is a requirement.

Step #3 — State what you want

What is it that you want? Why do you want to forgive? Are you looking for freedom? For peace? For a brighter future? For power?

Your answer is your goal. It doesn't matter what that goal is. You just need to know what you want out of this. That is because if your motivating WHY is strong enough, the HOW will take care of itself. You will find a way to reach your goal.

If your goal is to have a nightmare-free sleep and you haven't had that in 20 years, it will come to pass. When you are strongly motivated to do something, you will find a way over, under, or through every mountain to see it happen!

Perhaps it is something you do NOT want that drives you to forgive. Maybe you don't want to be like your parents or grandparents who couldn't forgive and lived miserable lives. Again, it doesn't matter what motivates you to forgive as long as you decide what you want.

Any answer is a good answer, as long as it drives you to take action and forgive.

Step #4 — Choose to forgive

Forgiveness is a choice. It always is. By choosing to forgive, you are deciding what you want to do with your hurt. Instead of letting bitterness fester, you are deciding that you want to put the issue to rest.

The fact that you are choosing to forgive automatically puts you in control. It is an important revelation and a significant part of the forgiveness process. The fact that you are in control every step of the way will help dispel any feelings that you are at the offender's mercy.

> *Forgiveness is not only mental; it is also a spiritual event.*

Some twisted people will taunt those they have hurt. Maybe you have endured this twisted type of abuse. When you take control, the offender has nothing on you. You are free! You are the victor, not the victim.

After all, you are the one choosing to forgive.

Step #5 — Verbalize your forgiveness

It's time to get verbal. Much of the forgiveness process to this point has been internal. Now it's time to speak out. With the person you are choosing to forgive and the incident clear in your mind, declare, "*I forgive you for what you did. I release you. I declare I am free!*"

Feel free to say this many times, but know that the process has begun. Forgiveness is not only mental; it is also a spiritual event. Things are moving and changing because of the words that come out of your mouth.

Will you feel different? Maybe. Do you need to feel different? Of course not! Feelings and forgiveness have little in common. Forgiveness is an act of your will, while feelings are attached to your emotions and might be up today and down tomorrow. Forgiveness is a choice you make.

Speaking your forgiveness aloud is necessary. You are telling yourself that you are forgiving. This is good for your heart and mind to hear ... and then act upon.

It is at this point that the question often arises, *"Should I also tell the person who hurt me that I have forgiven him?"*

Occasionally it is appropriate, but you must be VERY careful here. You might simply be adding more fuel to the fire, instigating a fresh wave of anger, resentment, and abuse. Or you might confuse the person, since most people who hurt us don't even know they have. But most likely, the other person will simply misunderstand you, which could be setting you up for a fall.

If you really feel you should verbalize your forgiveness to the person who hurt you, then do this:

• ***First***, make sure your attitude is right. If you have any pride, selfishness, or manipulative intent, it will be instantly visible and you will have a fiasco on your hands. Self-examine very carefully.

• ***Second***, ask one trusted confidant if it is wise, given the situation and the offending person, to communicate your forgiveness. Listen carefully to the advice you receive.

• ***Third***, pray about it. Psalm 34:14 says, *"Seek peace and pursue it."* If you are not at peace, then don't proceed. Ask God to help you know what to do and what to say.

• ***Fourth***, very humbly approach the person who hurt you and say something to this effect, *"I was hurt when you did/said ______. I want you to know that I am not angry with you. I forgive you and release you. I wish you the best."*

Again, you must be completely sure that this is the right thing to do and extremely careful with what you say. That is because most people do not understand forgiveness—**there is little doubt that the person who hurt you does NOT understand forgiveness**—and therefore will probably not understand what you are saying.

Consider the typical abusive husband who has been kicked out of the house. If you tell him, *"I forgive you,"* he hears, *"All is fine, come back home."* The neighbor who has had a running feud with you will probably hear, *"I'm better than you."* The sibling might hear, *"You're a loser."* **You simply don't know what the other person will hear.**

Usually, the best thing to do is to let the offending person see your forgiveness. You won't have to say anything.

Step #6 — Cover the offense

Part of forgiveness is burying the offense. There is a mini-funeral of sorts and you lay to rest the wrong that has been done to you.

In choosing to forgive, you give up your right to use the offense as leverage to get something from the person who hurt you. What's more, you should not tell others about how you were hurt. The issue is gone. You buried it. Now leave it alone.

But what if the pain is still very real? What if you feel the ongoing effects of the damage that was done? The answer is the same. You buried the offense, so don't dig it back up.

Covering the offense is smart for two very good reasons:

• ***First***, the more you talk about and dwell upon how you have been hurt, the greater the hurt will become. It's like feeding a fire with dry wood, paper, and even gasoline. The less you talk about it, the less you will think about it, and the less it will control your life.

• ***Second***, when you choose to forgive, you are choosing to cover the offense. Proverbs 10:12 says, *"Love covers over all wrongs."* Of course, this doesn't mean you are condoning or approving the behavior. Rather, it means that the offending person is guilty and you know it, but because you have chosen to extend forgiveness, you are covering the offense.

Not only does covering the offense protect you from continually reliving the past, it also protects the person who hurt you. They are able to move forward (if they want to), knowing that you won't be slapping them in the face with what they did. After all, if you were the one seeking forgiveness, wouldn't it be nice to know that the issue was dead and gone?

By covering an offense, everyone wins!

Step #7 — Show love

When you choose to forgive someone, you are in control. That is how you are able to show them love, no matter what they have done to you.

How do you show love to the person who hurt you? It depends on your situation, but it can be as simple as a smile, a "hi" in the elevator, or a card at Christmas. It might be an invitation to lunch or a gift for a certain accomplishment. You decide what you can do to show love.

Consider the neighbor who continued to shovel the snow off old cantankerous Mrs. Miller's sidewalk. He didn't need to do it and she certainly was not deserving of his kindness, considering that all she had to say were negative things about the neighbor's teenage sons. The neighbor did it because he forgave her and wanted to show love.

> *Part of showing love is helping the other person be free.*

Part of showing love is helping the other person be free. For example, let's say Mrs. Miller is your neighbor and she realizes how much of a pain she has been, and since you are her neighbor, you can't simply ignore her. When you talk, you can show her love by helping her feel good about herself. If she apologizes for being a grump, she might be afraid that you will repay her for her unkindness. Ease her fears by giving her your phone number and letting her know that you will always be there if she needs you. Or you might tell her that you'll be cleaning her sidewalk after the next big snow. In whatever you say, help her be free.

By showing love, you are giving the offending person permission to change. That is an important part of forgiveness.

Step #8 — Pray for them

By praying for the person who hurt you, you are pushing your forgiveness to the next level. This is good for you, and it is necessary!

Scripture says, *"Pray for those who persecute you"* (Matthew 5:44). **Why in the world should we pray for those who persecute us?** This is not an effort in futility or a task to do grudgingly. We should pray for the very people who hurt us because forgiveness is a practical issue as well as a spiritual issue.

When you choose to forgive, you take certain steps that are entirely down to earth, such as verbalizing your forgiveness and looking for ways to cover the offense. But your self-determination, as strong as it might be, isn't the whole answer.

> *Prayer reveals what's in the heart.*

At the spiritual level, you are dealing with your soul, your conscience, and your communication with God. **There is no way you can hide unforgiveness at this level!** If your forgiveness is genuine, you will know it, and if there is something else you need to deal with, you will know it. Prayer reveals what's in the heart.

In addition, by praying for the person who hurt you, you are giving God freedom to work in that person's life. You never know what might happen, but it's not your responsibility anyway.

Would it be okay with you if:

- The employee who stole $10,000 from you starts his own business and immediately turns a profit?
- Your ex-boyfriend gets married before you do?
- The drunk driver who killed your daughter gets out of jail?
- Your boss who fired you gets promoted?
- The individual who left your church starts his own church, and a lot of people leave to join him?

On the flip side, what if the person gets very sick, loses everything, suffers bankruptcy, or dies? Would you feel guilty? Would you feel partly responsible? Or would you secretly rejoice?

God will do as He sees fit. That is the bottom line.

You might be wondering, "*What exactly should I be praying?*" Most likely, your prayers will change over time, but you might begin by praying that God would bless the one who hurt you. You might pray that God would open your offender's eyes to see what he or she has done. Maybe you'll pray that your relationship will be restored.

> *You are not doing anything wrong by standing up for what you believe in!*

Through prayer, you are coming to terms with this as you truly release the person who hurt you. You are letting go. What happens next to that person is not your concern. You are free.

What a great reason to pray for your offender!

Step #9 — Look for reconciliation if possible

Having a relationship restored through forgiveness is absolutely wonderful! Futures are changed for the better, peace abounds, joy fills the air, and hope again is kindled in people's hearts.

Though reconciliation is the ideal, you cannot force it to happen. Do pray for it, but don't put pressure on the other person. That is because **it takes one person to forgive, but two people to mend a relationship.**

Monty is a good example. He had been hurt many times by his mother, to the point that he no longer wanted to talk to her. Though he lived close by, he didn't want anything to do with her. His unforgiveness was a very real wall around him.

Then one day a Christian businessman pointedly said to Monty, "You would not be who you are today if it were not for the good your mother instilled in you. Besides, have you walked a mile in her moccasins? I'm not justifying her actions, I'm just saying that you need to extend forgiveness and do your part to wipe the slate clean."

Monty wrestled with these challenging words for a few days, then drove over to his mom's house. They talked heart to heart for the first time in years. They cried together and they laughed together.

His mom reached out too, doing her part to restore the relationship. "I want to tell you a story that I've purposefully never told you before," she said to Monty. "When I was a junior in high school, I came home one day to find some doctors taking my mother away. They said she was sick and needed some help. Later, I learned they had taken her to a psychiatric hospital and given her shock treatment. She was gone. All the responsibility of raising my two brothers rested on me. Dad was an alcoholic and wouldn't lift a finger, so I had to make breakfast, lunch, and dinner, help with the homework, clean everyone's clothes, and more. I just wanted to be a daughter. I wanted my mother back."

Since their initial meeting, Monty and his mom have had numerous meals together, laughing and enjoying each other's company. "I forgave her and now feel better physically, mentally, and spiritually," he says. "I have come to see that we are both children of the same loving Father in heaven."

The healing between Monty and his mother ran so deep that he cancelled his Christmas plans (going to an island in Florida with friends) and spent Christmas with his mother. "It has been a dream of hers for many years to have me spend the night with her on Christmas Eve and wake up Christmas morning together," he explains. "It was a real blessing to both of us to spend Christmas together."

Again, because reconciliation involves two people, not every relationship can be salvaged. Try to communicate and clear the air, if you are able to. But remember that there is always a limit to what you can do. That is because the "majority vote" for reconciliation rests in the hands of the offending party. You cannot bring it about by yourself.

Forgive, look for reconciliation, but move on with your life at the same time. You must.

Step #10 — Move on

This day has come. It is time. You have forgiven, released, and prayed for the person who hurt you. You have done your best to bring restoration. ***Now, it is time to move on!***

The person who hurt you is in the past. If he or she won't come with you to the future, then move on and don't look back. Walk boldly forward into your bright future. You deserve to be there.

Decide what you want and focus your energy on getting there. You are free! What are you going to do with yourself?

- Are you going to go back to college?
- Are you going to write the book you've always wanted to write?
- Are you going to get remarried?
- Are you going to move to another city?
- Are you going to have another child?
- Are you going to start your own business?
- Are you going to keep doing what you've always been doing?

What is it that you most desire? Fix your sights on your goal and go for it! Life is too short to spend another minute being minimized in any way.

If you need to throw away photos, sell the house, or burn letters in order to cut ties with your past, then do it. This is your time. You have completed the steps to forgiveness.

Now, move on!

Have you really forgiven?

How do you know when you have forgiven the person who hurt you? Before you start doing an intense self-examination, remember what forgiveness is and is not. Here's a recap.

What forgiveness is:

- Acknowledging the hurt
- Keeping your eyes open

- Showing mercy
- Keeping no record of wrongs
- Living free from bitterness
- Taking responsibility
- Being honest about reality
- An attitude
- A lifestyle

What forgiveness is NOT:

- Approval
- Forgetting
- Justifying
- An obligation
- Giving in
- Reconciliation (restoration)
- Re-hiring
- Trust
- Getting even

Now, with that said, here are a few very important questions:

Q: *"Have you really forgiven someone if you remember what happened?"* Since forgiveness is not forgetting, then just because you remember does not mean you have unforgiveness in your heart.

Q: *"Have you really forgiven if you won't let a lying, cheating, abusive person back into your life?"* Since forgiveness is not approval, then standing your ground for what is right does not mean you have unforgiveness in your heart.

Q: *"Have you really forgiven if you won't trust the person who hurt you?"* Since forgiveness is not trust, then keeping your guard up does not mean you have unforgiveness in your heart.

Whatever your question, see how it measures up to the definition of forgiveness. If it doesn't line up, then toss it out. You are not doing anything wrong by standing up for what you believe in!

And if you are still concerned that you might not have forgiven someone, you probably already have. Our minds and emotions have been programmed one way, and if forgiveness is new to you, then it will take a while for your new reality to replace your old reality.

Or maybe you want to start back with step #1 and work your way to step #10. You are learning to forgive, so repetition is a good thing. That's fine. Rewind as many times as necessary.

Don't let yourself feel bad if you think you haven't mastered the art of forgiveness. The fact that you are trying to forgive should be reason enough to celebrate! You are taking control, standing up, courageously facing a difficult situation ... and conquering it!

Be patient with yourself as you learn to walk in forgiveness.

It is important to recognize that God wants you to walk in the benefits of forgiveness and that Satan wants you to remain bitter, full of hatred, and confused. While writing about forgiveness and the attacks of Satan, the Apostle Paul proclaimed, "*We are not unaware of his schemes*" (II Corinthians 2:11).

Because forgiveness is so powerful, both naturally and spiritually, you can expect there to be a battle, but it is a battle that you will win!

When you know you have forgiven

When it comes right down to it, the absolute best way to determine if you have forgiven someone is to check the fruit. If you wonder what type of tree is growing in an orchard, you simply look at its fruit. Apples dangling from the branches will immediately answer any question you might have.

So it is with forgiveness.

Here is the "fruit" test. **Have you seen, felt, enjoyed, or experienced any of these in your life since you chose to forgive:**

Peace
Joy
Health
Strength

Freedom
Power
Gratefulness
Restoration
Growth
A brighter future
Money
Time together with family
A clean conscience
Hope
A better relationship with God
Self-control
Creativity
Energy
Sleep
Advancement
Passion
Contentment
Communication with loved ones
Increased opportunity
Justice

Have you found any of these in your life? Most likely you have, and more than one. That is what forgiveness looks like, smells like, and tastes like. That is the fruit of forgiveness. Enjoy it!

Putting forgiveness to work in my own life

A few years ago, I experienced the "acid test" of forgiveness. I had borrowed some money from a local bank, putting up controlling interest in my parent company as collateral. The bank note, like all bank notes for the past 50 years, never was late and was often paid early. So, I was stunned to get a call from the local bank, demanding payment in full in 30 days! If I did not comply, I would lose the stock in my company. Naturally, I called the banker, but he wouldn't budge. I asked if I could have 60 days to transfer the note.

"No," was his curt reply.

His attorney called me next. I was pleased to speak with his attorney because he happened to be my Sunday school teacher and had been a friend for many years. "Mike, tell the banker what you know of me," I requested. "It doesn't make sense that he'd call the loan for no reason whatsoever."

Mike replied, "I'm sorry, there is nothing I can do on this one. He's made up his mind and he won't change. He simply doesn't like you."

I scrambled, and I mean scrambled! I sold raw land (which has since increased in value over 500%) and I sold apartment complexes (which would have paid for themselves by now). After 26 days, I could only come up with 80% of what was needed to pay off the loan. Thankfully, another local banker called and said, "I heard what has happened. How can we help? You can always bank with us."

That was good news! I borrowed the remaining 20% and closed out my loan at the first bank. I lost a lot of money in the deal, all for no reason. But sadly, the banker who gave me such a hard time has since lost his good name, his wife, and his business. His personal problems consumed him. I think I just happened to get caught in the mix.

I chose to forgive and moved on.

CHAPTER FOUR

Forgiving Others

An everyday occurrence!

Ignoring issues never makes them go away. This is especially true when it involves family. Unresolved hurts breed bitterness that affects everyone. There is no escaping the silence, the awkwardness, and the loss of intimacy. The only way to fix it is by coming to terms with the pain ... and choosing to forgive.

The story below is from a grown daughter who had a change of heart and chose to forgive her aging father.

A change of heart

A lifetime of abuse at the hands of my father left me full of bitterness, anger, and hatred. When the years of sexual abuse came to a halt, the physical and emotional abuse began. I learned to trust absolutely no one, sometimes not even myself. I used to say, "The only reason I would attend my father's funeral would be to assure myself that he was dead." I hated the man!

In October of 1998, at the age of 41, I had a life-changing encounter with Jesus Christ. He forgave me for all of my sins and did not hold any against me! It was wonderful!

Forgiving the man who abused me, however, was not in the cards. I felt that God would understand why I didn't, couldn't, and wouldn't forgive my father because of how much I had suffered.

But the more I grew in God's Word and the more I learned of His absolute forgiveness, the more I realized that forgiveness is not a feeling. God requires us to forgive others, and He does not make any exceptions for the degree to which we have been offended. Matthew 6:14-15 says, *"For if you forgive men when they sin against you, your heavenly Father will also forgive you. But if you do not forgive men their sins, your Father will not forgive your sins."*

I knew that I had to forgive my father, but I sure didn't feel forgiveness for him. I prayed to God, "I, Renee, release my father into your loving arms. Please release me from the bondage of unforgiveness." God heard my prayer and began to work in all of our lives.

About three years later, my father had a stroke and the decision was made that he would go to a long-term care facility and that my mother would come to live with my husband and me. Jeff and I had been married for less than a year, but he assured me that it would be fine.

Three months later, the long-term care facility called to say that my father was not able to stay there. I was terrified! My mother had already moved in with us. Would I have to allow my father to move in as well? Again, Jeff said it would work out. I didn't believe him. How could having my father living under the same roof be fine?

My father moved in with us. Jeff and I learned how to manage, but it wasn't an easy time. I'm sure that my parents also would have preferred to be in their own home, but God knew things we did not.

Just before Christmas, five months after my Father moved into our home, we were hit by another vehicle on the way to church. My mother was killed instantly.

It was heartbreaking to hear my father talk about the woman with whom he had spent over 60 years of his life. How much he missed her! I noticed my attitude toward my father was beginning to change. Forgiveness was beginning to take hold.

A few weeks later, my father received Jesus as his personal Savior and was baptized at our church. He was 84 years old! He was a changed man. My father lived with us for another year and a half. When he died, things were different at the funeral than I had imagined. I actually missed him! And I was experiencing a joy that I never expected; my father was in Heaven!

I am so thankful that God allowed me to have that time with my father. It was a time of healing for the both of us, and I know that it will have an impact on my family for generations to come.

I learned that forgiveness does not mean we have to allow ourselves to be mistreated in any way. Forgiveness does not mean that my father's actions were right or that I had to trust him completely. Forgiveness does mean that we allow God to work in our lives and in the lives of the people against whom we hold bitterness.

Forgiving my father has brought wonderful blessings to my life!

Forgiveness is a necessity

That you need to forgive is a given. If you are alive, you've been hurt by other people. That's just what happens. People hurt other people, sometimes intentionally, but most often unintentionally.

What do you do with the hurt and pain? How do you deal with it? Can you get on with your life? Will you?

Since you have no doubt experienced the need to forgive others, the question to ask is, "*Have you forgiven them?*"

You have already read the steps to forgiveness from the last chapter. You know exactly how to forgive. But can you forgive? **Do you really want to forgive?**

Most people do. Here are nine reasons why you *want* to forgive those who hurt you:

Reason #1— You want control

"When we blame another person for how we feel, we grant them the power to regulate our emotions," says Dr. Fred Luskin.

> *You are taking responsibilitu for yourself, and that is how you gain control.*

Do you want to give someone else, much less the person who hurt you, any control over your life? Of course not! You want control, so take it.

Sitting and waiting for justice or an apology is another way of giving up power and control. Some people wait on the person who hurt them to come back and fix the situation. It isn't going to happen! Joyce Meyer, a well-known speaker and author, was abused in countless ways as a child. She now says, "I was looking to people to pay me back when I should have been looking to God."

If you want control, you have to take it. It will never come by blaming others or by waiting for it to happen. **The sheer act of forgiveness is power.** You have to take responsibility for yourself. You are not taking responsibility for what happened to you. You are taking responsibility for yourself, and that is how you gain control.

Reason #2— You want peace

Peace is a wonderful thing! It's good for the heart, mind, soul, and body. Those who need to forgive also need peace, **for where there is no forgiveness there is no peace**.

Actually, if you are hungry for peace, it has moved from a "good idea" to a strong desire. You must have it! When that is the case, it is much easier to extend forgiveness. The peace you desire becomes more important than the hurt and pain.

When you must have peace, you will do whatever it takes to get it.

Reason #3 — You want to move on

No doubt you have heard unforgiving people tell you again and again about things that happened to them many months or years ago. The hurt is real, nobody is denying that, but when it's all they talk about, doesn't it get tiring? They need to move on, but by their own willful decisions, they remain trapped in their pasts.

Not so with you! You want to move on, to get past the hurt and to move beyond the pain. The only way to do that is through forgiveness. It might not be the most popular thing to do, but when you are sufficiently tired of being where you have been, you will cut the chains that have anchored you to your past. My pastor, Michael Toby, aptly describes forgiveness as "unhooking yourself from the offender." Forgive and let it go so you can move on!

Forgiveness does not remove the incident from your memory, but it does cut the chains that bind you to that memory.

Bishop Desmund Tutu noted, "Forgiveness does not mean condoning what has been done. It means taking what happened seriously and not minimizing it; drawing out the sting in the memory that threatens to poison our entire existence."

Forgiveness does not remove the incident from your memory, but it does cut the chains that bind you to that memory. That is freedom and that is why you want to move on.

Reason #4 — You want to stop being a doormat

Forgiveness is calling a spade a spade. It's about being real and honest. As you know, forgiveness is acknowledging the hurt with eyes wide open and is not denial, trust, or giving in.

It is God's desire that you walk free and live whole. He does not want you to be stepped on, run over, scraped up, and abused. When you stand up and address an issue, you are proclaiming, *"I am a person, not a doormat. Get off of me!"*

Forgiveness gives you the power to do just that. The change will be a process, as it involves your own thoughts and actions, but what others say about you has no place. You are not a doormat!

Reason #5 — You want to avoid bitterness

Unforgiveness breeds bitterness. Everyone who is unforgiving is also bitter. It might be more obvious in some people than it is in others, but unforgiveness and bitterness go hand in hand. You can't have one without the other.

The thing about bitterness is that it spreads like yeast, fire, acid, and the plague, all mixed into one. You cannot escape its impact on your life. Scripture says, *"Get rid of all bitterness"* (Ephesians 4:31), and for good reason! Bitterness will spoil everything good in your life. It will ruin friendships, relationships, minds, hearts, emotions, and futures. **There is nothing redeemable about bitterness.** Get rid of it now!

> *"Those who refuse to forgive carry bitterness and anger with them to the grave. Even while they live, they live without joy or peace."*
> – *Dana Chau*

"But I was wronged," or *"I want justice,"* people say. As nice as it would be to get what you want and rightly deserve, the odds are not in your favor. Most likely, the person who hurt you is never going to apologize and justice is not going to be served. Are you going to wait around for it to happen?

Those who wait have not forgiven, and those who have not forgiven are bitter. If you want to avoid bitterness, step forward and forgive. Let it go. If you ever get an apology or justice, be thankful, but recognize that you don't need it. You have forgiveness.

Reason #6 — You want to be whole

Did the person who hurt you take something of value from you? What did you lose? A loved one? Your virginity? Your money? Your home? Your peace of mind? Your innocence?

If you have lost something, forgiveness is the only way to get it back. Unforgiveness acts as a magnifying glass, always showing us how big our need is, how large the wound is, and how massive the loss is.

Forgiveness has the incredible ability to bring healing in every area: emotionally, physically, mentally, and spiritually. Only when you are whole are you able to reach your full potential. Choose forgiveness.

Reason #7 — You want to love

Can you love if you have a heart full of unforgiveness? Those who are holding unforgiveness toward someone might argue that they can show love, but ask those who have forgiven and you'll hear a different story.

Elisa is a good example. An adult (a friend of her parents) sexually abused her when she was only three years old. When she was almost 30 years old, she stated, "I've never been able to establish a lasting relationship with a man. What happened to me scarred me for life."

She wants desperately to love, but she isn't able to. For some, it is impossible to show or receive love, affection, hugs, kisses, or touches. Others have trust, respect, or authority issues. Is unforgiveness the cause? In many cases, it is.

I've found that people who have the proverbial "chip on the shoulder" have unforgiveness in their lives. They are living hostile lives in which they are combative, confrontational, and controlling. Sadly, it is humanly impossible for them to have peace, joy, or happiness, no matter what they do. It will not work. The chip will never leave their shoulder until they forgive.

Whatever the issue, refusing to forgive is not going to fix anything. It might take some time and effort to work through the process of forgiveness, but it's certainly worth it!

If you want to love, then forgive.

Reason #8 — You want to break the cycle

It is strange, and we are inclined to believe it unlikely, but people who have been hurt have an uncanny way of repeating the same offense. There are countless stories of abused children growing up and abusing their own children. Why is that? Didn't it hurt enough the first time? Why would they then pass it on to the next generation? To their own children!

> *Those who forgive seldom, if ever, repeat the offense.*

Hurting people will hurt other people. It's a cycle. Some repeat out of spite and anger, while others don't know why they become what they hate. In the end, it makes no difference. The cycle continues.

You can stand up and break the cycle! This is exactly the motivation many people have for choosing to forgive. Those who forgive seldom, if ever, repeat the offense. Isn't that enough reason to forgive right there?

In fact, those who forgive, battling through pain, inabilities, insecurities, and hurt, often help others forgive. This concept is seen in the many ministries and charities run by the very people who once needed help themselves. Halfway houses are run by ex-cons, substance abuse centers are run by former drug addicts, homeless shelters are run by people who used to live on the streets, etc. Forgiveness has a way of restoring much more than was taken!

To forgive is to break the cycle.

Reason #9 — You want to improve your relationship with God

Unforgiveness affects your relationship with everyone ... and with God. Author and pastor Charles Stanley points out, "Few things in life have the devastating, corroding, collapsing effect of an unforgiving spirit. An unforgiving spirit affects your body, your emotions, your mind, your relationships, your work, your goals, your effectiveness in your Christian life, your witness, and the power of the Holy Spirit in your life. There is no way to have an unforgiving spirit without it corroding and disintegrating something within you of great value."

The moral of the story is simple: forgive so that you are free of an unforgiving spirit! Pastor Joel Osteen teaches, "Unforgiveness stops the flow of God's anointing in our lives."

What hurt or pain is worth holding onto that minimizes you in every way? Really! Is anything worth that price? Never!

Having unforgiveness in your heart does not mean that you have no relationship with God. That is not the issue. The issue is improving your relationship with God. When my sister finally forgave our dad, she called me and said, "I have peace that truly passes understanding. It's beautiful! I've never had it before."

How could a mature Christian who genuinely loved God, had a servant's heart, and cared deeply for others say such a thing? Here is the answer: Only when you forgive will you see what you've been missing.

Forgiving those who hurt you

You really do want to forgive. I commend you. Well done. After you choose to forgive, the next step is simple: **actually do it.**

This requires that you take action. Forgiveness is all about taking action, much of which is one-sided. You will do most, if not all, of the work. (As you know, forgiveness requires one person, while restoration requires two.)

To forgive those who have hurt you, apply the same 10 steps we discussed earlier:

Step #1 — ***Decide on the hurt***
Step #2 — ***Be real, be honest***
Step #3 — ***State what you want***
Step #4 — ***Choose to forgive***
Step #5 — ***Verbalize your forgiveness***
Step #6 — ***Cover the offense***
Step #7 — ***Show love***
Step #8 — ***Pray for them***
Step #9 — ***Look for reconciliation if possible***
Step #10 — ***Move on***

> *Forgiveness requires one person, while restoration requires two.*

That is what it takes to forgive those who have hurt you. One step might take longer than another, and that's fine. You might even want to "start over" with the steps as you are working to forgive some people, but the process of forgiveness has started. You can be confident in that.

Take extra care with family

Where do we feel the effects of forgiveness and unforgiveness the most? Without question, it is within our families!

Were you one of those children who tried to keep the peace between family members when they were arguing? Did you try to make everyone happy when someone pulled the "silent treatment"? Did you feel the tension of unforgiveness in the air?

As an adult, have you ever wondered how you managed to end up with the family you did? How could siblings be so different? Why are some of the longest-lasting disagreements between family members?

> *If you are still holding unforgiveness in your heart toward someone, it's costing you more than it's costing them.*

No matter what is said and done, you are still part of the same family. You can't do anything about it. Families need forgiveness like travelers in the desert need water!

Forgiveness is a must within families, which is why it is incredibly important that we take extra care to resolve issues and keep short accounts. Taking extra care is about taking the offensive. If you said or did something in the past that hurt someone in the family, has the issue been resolved? Has the other person forgiven you? Have you asked for forgiveness?

In addition to fixing what *you know* you've broken, **there is a time and a place within your family to fix the things *you don't know* you've broken.** How can you repair the damage caused by what you said or did if you don't remember what you said or did?

Simple: **you ask.** You don't remember, but they do!

To your spouse and each child, ask plainly, *"Have I ever said something or done something to you that hurt you or made you feel rejected?"*

Then listen attentively to what they say ... and apologize! Ask for forgiveness right there. Make restitution if you need to.

It might be a "little" thing, but little things can grow into big mountains. By fixing the hurts and pains, you are taking the offensive and making sure that unforgiveness—**and everything else that comes with it**—does not grow in your family.

It doesn't matter how old your children are. I know a 40-year-old son who still wishes his dad had come to his basketball games. It seems silly that it is still important 25 years later, but each person is different. The hurt is still there.

Make restitution if you need to.

You simply cannot know how a word or deed affects someone else. By asking, you can right the wrong. Among family, this is a must.

Doing what is good for you

When all is said and done, forgiving others is incredibly good for you, while not forgiving others is incredibly bad for you. **What else is there to say?**

I know you'll make the right decision.

Putting forgiveness to work in my own life

In sales, no matter what I was selling, I was second to none. I couldn't be beaten. I wouldn't be beaten. When I joined a Georgia insurance company, I went right to work, adding over 800 salespeople to the team within a year. We were producing a massive amount of sales. I was 27 and already a millionaire.

My partner in the agency (35 years my senior), unbeknownst to me, was cheating every step of the way. When we bought a plane together, he double charged me so that I ended up paying for his half as well as my half. He had two sets of books: one to show me and one for the business.

Then one Monday morning I showed up at the office to find everything gone, completely cleared out! There was not a single chair, filing cabinet, or piece of paper left behind. All the money was gone and I was left holding the bag!

I helped the several hundred salespeople I had recruited find other jobs. It took 18 months to clean up his mess. I ended up broke, but content that I had done the right thing.

My partner had no remorse and moved to Alabama to further distance himself from the business. I forgave him and chose to start over. Interestingly, he died of heart failure within the year at age 48.

And the million dollars that I lost? I have since made that back, hundreds of times over!

CHAPTER FIVE

Forgiving God

If you need to!

Being real. That is one of the most important, yet difficult, things to do at certain times in our lives. I received this true story from an incredibly real, incredibly honest, husband and wife in Florida. His story is first; her story comes at the end of this chapter.

Did she have to die?

My daughter, Diane, was a vivacious, outgoing, beautiful, mature, young lady. She loved God with all her heart, went on mission trips, and worked with the youth in our church. At age 21, she married the love of her life. But one year and nine months later, Diane was dead from cancer.

When she was first diagnosed, I felt like I heard two clear words from God, clear as I've ever heard anything before. The first was, "Honor your father and your mother and you will have long life on the earth." Since Diane was just 22 years old, I figured she had plenty of time to live.

The second word I heard was, "This is not a sickness unto death."

Based on those two words, I was confident that the sickness was a process that we would walk through. It wasn't going to result in her death, and God was going to be glorified. Up until the week before she died, I wasn't worried about it. I prayed, fasted, and took care of her, but I was not thinking about her dying. I wasn't going to lose my daughter.

That last week, I told God, "Unless you intervene here, unless you supernaturally heal her, she's going to die." I could see her getting sicker by the day. On Thursday evening (she died on Sunday), I was working with the youth group at our church as normal. Diane spoke that night. She told stories, talked to the kids, and encouraged them.

On Friday, she talked just a bit, but after that, she hardly said another word. On Saturday, she barely moved. On Sunday, I held her in her favorite big easy chair. As I rocked her, I told her I loved her and prayed for her many times, but she was getting less and less responsive. We called EMS and rode with her in the ambulance to the hospital.

The doctors did their best to ease her pain, but there was little they could do. She died a few hours later. Her heart quit, and she was gone.

My eldest daughter was dead at the young age of 22. Questions swirled in my mind:

• **Why didn't the two words I heard from God line up with reality?** I can't explain it. I know that I heard the words from God, but I can't explain it. It isn't what happened and I don't have an explanation for it.

• **Was I wrong to believe those two words?** The two words I believe I heard were not against God's Word, and they gave me peace to walk through a very hard time. They also gave me faith to walk the rest of my life with Him. Do I understand it all? No, but I'm okay with that.

• **Why did Diane die?** I know Satan comes to steal, kill, and destroy and that all good things come from God. Diane's death was obviously not from God. Satan stole her from us. I don't know why she died.

• **Could God not have healed her?** God has the power. He can change anything in a moment. He could have miraculously healed her, but He didn't. He didn't fail because He is perfect. If there is a failure, then it must be something else. My wife said, "God has the power to heal, yet He didn't. Why is that?" I don't have a good answer.

• **Did I not have enough faith?** I struggled with my lack of faith. I don't believe my faith was at the level that would have allowed the miracle to take place. I blamed myself more than anyone or anything. I might be wrong about this, but that's my view.

• **Is God to blame?** I know without a doubt that God is not to blame. I have to believe that God is good. I have to be able to trust Him. No matter what I see and what happens and how I feel and what my emotions are, do I believe in God? Yes, I do. That's the bottom line.

I don't blame God for the death of my daughter. I certainly don't like what happened, much less understand it, but I'm okay with that. I know God loves me and I trust Him.

Can you forgive God?

The process of forgiveness begins with a specific hurt caused by a specific person. The only person you need to forgive is the person who hurt you. Right? And if someone didn't hurt you, there is no need for forgiveness.

To forgive God means that He did something hurtful that warrants forgiveness. True? Let's take a second to review a few details about God. He is:

Holy
Perfect
All powerful
All knowing
Loving
Kind
Giving
Merciful
Compassionate
Our healer
Our provider
Our deliverer
Our protector
Our comforter
Our Savior
Madly in love with us (He gave His only Son for us!)
Perfect (just so we don't forget)

With that said, what is it that God needs to be forgiven for? What has He done wrong? The only thing that seems questionable is His over-the-top, unstoppable love, mercy, kindness, and belief in us!

Now, is it logically possible that the God of the universe, who is everything good incarnate, would purposefully and maliciously hurt you? I don't think so. (I'm not saying your hurt is not real, I'm just saying that God did not do it.)

Is it possible that you might experience hurt and pain in life that you cannot attribute to another person? Certainly. Does that automatically make God responsible? No.

> *"God wants us to be real and honest. If we don't understand, that's okay."*
> *– Pat O'Conner*

Therefore, if God is not responsible for what happened to you, you cannot forgive Him, just like you cannot forgive someone who didn't hurt you. It's not possible. There is nothing to forgive.

Can you blame God?

You can blame anyone for anything you want. You can even blame God for things He didn't do. Consider Diane's parents who watched her die at age 22 from cancer. They could have blamed God, but would that have meant He did it? **No, because blame does not make someone responsible.**

The truth is, we are free to blame God for anything and everything, but does that mean He did it? Of course not!

Are you blaming God for something? Let's say your business is going bankrupt. Can you blame it on God? Sure you can, but you are wasting your time. What you need to do is learn from what is happening. Is the financial demise of your business your responsibility, the result of something beyond your control, or something else? Hold off on applying blame. It doesn't do you any good.

What about the innocent who suffer? Little children starve to death every day, and God is blamed. Is it His fault? No, it is not His fault. We humans are doing it to ourselves. We can't place the responsibility of feeding our own children or taking care of those less fortunate on God. It's our job, not His, which means He is not to blame.

The truth is, we are free to blame God for anything and everything, but does that mean He did it?

What about natural disasters? Who else is to blame when the only tree in your yard falls on your house and kills your child, or your trailer is the only trailer destroyed by a twister, or lightning strikes your son and grandson while they are walking to church.

Things happen that don't make sense, but does that mean that God did it? No. You can blame God all you want, but that doesn't mean He is responsible.

If you've blamed God

You have to come to a point in your life where you can say, *"I don't understand what happened, but I still trust you, God."* And if necessary, add, *"I forgive you, God. Please heal me."*

It will do you good to say it. Though technically you cannot forgive God because He is not responsible for your hurt or pain, it can do you good emotionally, spiritually, and mentally to tell Him that you forgive Him. If it helps you, then by all means do it.

As you know, the person who loses is the person who gets bitter. Release any bitterness that you have toward God. If you don't, it will drive a wedge between you and Him. Your relationship will stagnate and you will be miserable. And like a bothersome neighbor, you will try to avoid God at all costs.

Diane's father says, "To allow your relationship with God to grow, you may have to say, 'I forgive you, God,' 60,000 times. But know that when you say, 'Forgive me God for letting this separate us; please heal me,' God will do just that."

If you've blamed God, your relationship with Him is not what it could be. Forgive Him if you feel you need to, but do whatever it takes to release any bitterness that might have come between you. He will step in as well to help restore your relationship. That is, after all, what He wants the most!

Being real with God

If you have a lot of questions, that's fine. Ask them all! You might not get your answers, but ask them and keep on asking them until you have a peace about them. When that happens, don't worry about them anymore.

Here's the honest truth: **You have to be comfortable with the fact that God knows everything and you don't.** To want to know everything is to expect to be God, and that will never happen. Only God is God. There will be things you don't understand. Can you live with that? It's not like there is much choice, but you need to acknowledge that you are making that decision.

What's more, you cannot sit and wait for answers. The answers might never come. All God promises is that you will some day see clearly. You will eventually get it. You will understand, but it will either be here on earth or in heaven after you are dead. Can you live with that? Again, it's not like there is much choice, but you need to acknowledge that you are making that decision.

> *To want to know everything is to expect to be God, and that will never happen. Only God is God.*

The reality is that God desires to have a relationship with each one of us. We are the better for it, but if we allow unforgiveness and bitterness to grow in our hearts because of something we think God did, we lose!

Be 100% real with God. Tell Him everything. Your hurt and pain are real. Communicate. Don't hold back. Tell Him you forgive Him. Ask Him for forgiveness. Do whatever it takes.

When you are done, know that God loves you ... and that you can trust Him.

The second half of Diane's story—from her mother

Each individual grieves very differently. It held true for Pat and me. I couldn't understand how he was holding everything in check. I asked him once, "What are you doing with the pain?" He said, "I don't go there!" I couldn't imagine how he was so capable of putting it somewhere that was buried so deep that it did not affect his everyday life. Over the years I saw the devastation of that at work.

Pat blamed himself. I don't know why. I would ask him how Diane's dying could possibly be his fault. He said that if he possessed enough faith, he could have spared her from dying. He actually went to the crematory and laid hands on Diane's body and tried to raise her from the dead. If that's not faith, I don't know what is. I told him never to try that on me. Let me go be with God!

Our perceptions become our realities. This doesn't make it true, it just is. I am not a religious person. I am a person of faith. It doesn't matter that I don't see it; I believe what my heart confirms to be true.

One year before Diane's diagnosis, this word came to me: "Prepare for a season of 'suddenlies'!" I put it on my refrigerator, not knowing what was to come.

When Diane's diagnosis was given, I prayed. I made my request to God. We came home from the hospital after her lymph nodes were tested, and I went out to the clothesline to hang some laundry and to have a heart to heart with God. I cried—from fear of the unknown—and I cried out as a child would for her Daddy's help. I told Him that my request was for Him to heal Diane, but if He wasn't going to leave her here, my declaration was (despite the confusion and lack of understanding) that I would continue to live for Him. I knew I must do this, or I would be consumed in the Shadow of Death.

Later, I would have another conversation with God. I told Him, "I see you are not going to heal her—please take her quickly!" He obliged. I think Diane was not afraid to die. She was more afraid of how others would suffer. She was tired and opted out. She knew what lay ahead of her.

God received Diane. I don't think He took her. I don't believe Satan had anything to do with it either. Diane belonged to God and Satan had nothing in her. I believe Satan is powerless over those who belong to God, but he can work in a believer's life when we fail to walk in our God-given authority. He can't take anything; we can surrender to him. Satan gets blamed and credited for more than he should.

When Jesus said, "It is finished," He left us the Holy Spirit as a teacher, comforter, and source of wisdom. We need not fear the evil one. He is our footstool. This does not insure a perfect, pain-free life.

Life is one part faith, one part mystery, and one part adventure. It is for us to discover God, discover who we are in His family, and discover how we can love Him, love ourselves, and love others. When we miss the mark, it is no one's fault but our own. Blame is for the weak and ignorant.

I blame no one for anything. I forgive everyone, everything. Forgiveness is not pardon! Forgiveness is not acceptance. Forgiveness does not mean the person that wronged you will be spared the consequences of their actions. I can forgive the man who molested Diane and her cousins as a child, but his pardon is God's responsibility. Forgiveness does not make that person right; it makes me free.

I did not blame God for Diane's death. It was just a bizarre set of circumstances. Could the cancer be from a bug she got on a mission trip? Could it be from something she was exposed to in her environment? Could it be a result of the way her body responded to stress? I have no answers. I have peace.

What did I do with all the pain? Every moment I took a breath, I gave it to God. Over and over again ... it took five years for the severity to lessen. But through the pain, I found answers to questions that I've asked for years. I know God could have made lots of things happen through Diane's survival story, but instead, He showed me all the fruit that remained despite her death. I rejoice in that. For God's children, death is a doorway, not a dungeon.

It was a wake-up call. It was an opportunity to find out what is truly important in life and allow the trivial to pass by without so much as a minute's care. Her death set me free.

Was it hell? Yes! Did it leave scars? Yes! Did we survive? Yes! Now we turn and comfort others with the same comfort we were given. Words will not change a heart. Clichés will not change a heart. Your best religious intentions will not change a heart. Only love changes hearts.

One day, Diane said to me, "Cancer is just a circumstance, Mom." For the man who lost his job or the girl who has been abused or the family that doesn't know where they will get their next meal, these are all just circumstances. Mine is no different or worse than theirs.

Death is not the end; nor is it a punishment for a lack of faith. Diane is in paradise. That's all I know, and I will see her again one day. Until I do, I will rejoice in the fruit of her life and love every soul that God places in my life.

Putting forgiveness to work in my own life

One of my all-time best friends hurt me the worst. He was an incredibly talented individual who eventually ran several of my businesses in Florida. I even named him in my will as executor of my estate. He had my complete trust.

Then one day the auditors who had been working on my annual audit called me with the bad news, which turned out to be just the tip of the iceberg. Things were much worse than we could have even imagined. The more we dug, the more cover ups we found. It was an absolute mess! In the end, many people lost their jobs, I spent millions of dollars fixing what this individual had broken, and several of my businesses were significantly reduced in size.

With his self-serving leadership style, he made wrong decisions that hurt the company. In addition to the financial, business, and personnel losses, my trust had been utterly broken. I chose to forgive and even helped him financially a couple times, but the damage that was done could not be fixed. Of all the people who have left over the years, this is the individual I miss the most. He passed away not long ago, but I find myself thinking about him quite often.

Looking back, I believe that if I didn't practice forgiveness ... I would have lost everything by now.

CHAPTER SIX

Forgiving Yourself

An absolute must!

For most of us, forgiving others is easier than forgiving ourselves. We expect so much more of ourselves and assume that we should "know better." This is, however, no excuse. Forgiveness is to be given to everyone involved, yourself included!

Here, a young lady from California shares honestly her struggle to deal with her hurt, pain, disappointment, and unforgiveness toward herself.

Dumped for another girl

Stan was an incredible catch, or at least that's what I thought at first. After a few months of dating, giving him far more than I wanted to give, he dumped me. He wasted no time finding another girl, even chasing some of my friends. I was physically wracked with pain and confusion. Depression replaced my peace, sadness replaced my joy, and feelings of worthlessness replaced my positive self-image. Honestly, I was a mess.

Looking back, the months we spent together were a steady downward spiral for me. Stan had steadily chipped away at my core confidence and self-esteem, trying to make me into the crutch that he needed.

I'll say it plainly: Stan was a careless, selfish, self-centered, egotistical pig! But acknowledging his problems did not give me the help that I needed. I wanted to be free of him in every way.

To be free, I would have to forgive him. That would be a challenge. Even greater, however, would be forgiving myself. How could I have stooped so low? As a Christian, I should have known better. How could I have willingly given myself to this piece of scum?

Self-forgiveness was not going to be easy.

When Stan walked out on me, I got my life back. Yes, it hurt like crazy when he dumped me, but I'm glad he did. I worked on forgiving him little by little, day by day. I acknowledged the pain he caused me and made the bold declaration, "You hurt me, but I will not let you affect my life any longer. I forgive you and release you." I also took responsibility for my part in the disastrous relationship.

The process of forgiveness had begun, but it would take almost a year before I felt fully free of him. Seeing Stan at church with his new girlfriend was a stab in the back at first, but before long I found myself feeling sorry for both of them and actually wishing them the best. I knew I was free!

Forgiving myself? That was the hardest part. But I reached a point in my wallowing depression and self-pity when I had finally had enough. I wanted to live! I chose to forgive myself.

I've come a long way since Stan. I feel more confident, secure, and stronger than before. I have two jobs and am making more money than I've ever made before. I'm looking forward to my future again. I am in shape, eating healthy, enjoying time with my family and friends, and looking forward to some day getting married.

I'm in no rush to get married, that's for sure, but I'm at peace with myself. I am a better person today. I've taken responsibility, and I've forgiven myself. I have a great future ahead of me.

Mr. Right, wherever he is, is going to have to be one smart, loving, thoughtful, and strong man, or I'll have nothing to do with him. I should have known that before, but I'm thankful I learned it through forgiveness.

The top 13 reasons why forgiving yourself is hard

You've learned how to forgive others and you've learned how (if necessary) to forgive God. Now for the hard part: **forgiving yourself.**

For most people, forgiving themselves is a very difficult thing to do. Is that true for you? If so, why? Perhaps it is because:

1. You can justify the actions of others, but not your own.
2. You still feel guilty, regardless of what others say.
3. You cannot accept failure.
4. You have to live with yourself.
5. You cannot escape your past.
6. You can give grace, but you cannot receive it.
7. You couldn't possibly pay for what you did.
8. You feel it is your duty to punish yourself.
9. Your mind will not stop replaying the incident.
10. You don't feel worthy of forgiveness.
11. You don't believe others and God have really forgiven you.
12. You refuse to forgive others.
13. You simply don't know how.

Whatever the reason—or excuse—you still need to forgive yourself. It is important that you come to grips with that fact. I repeat: ***You need to forgive yourself.***

When you accept that, you can begin the actual process.

Why you need to forgive yourself

When you forgive yourself, you finish the circle of forgiveness. You complete the circuit. You are then completely free to enjoy all the benefits of forgiveness without the side effects of unforgiveness.

If you don't forgive yourself, however, the circle is incomplete. You are not finished. What's more, according to author R. T. Kendall, "There is no lasting joy in forgiveness if it doesn't include forgiving yourself." How very true!

> *Those who refuse to forgive others cannot forgive themselves.*

Forgiving yourself is a prerequisite to your success. Unforgiveness, whether toward someone, toward God, or toward yourself is one of the surest ways to sabotage your success. In fact, **unforgiveness that is self-directed will do more damage than any other form of unforgiveness!**

To move beyond, to reach the next level, you need to release yourself! Author D. Patrick Miller says, "When you first decide to forgive yourself, you are stepping upon a great escalator headed up toward your potential." I like that analogy.

On your way toward reaching your full potential, forgive yourself.

The freedom in forgiving yourself

Unforgiveness is self-inflicted bondage, plain and simple. It really doesn't matter if your unforgiveness is directed toward others, God, or yourself: You are still in bondage if you don't forgive.

Forgiveness brings freedom. Here is what you gain by forgiving yourself:

Freedom #1— Freedom to be at peace

There can only be peace in your heart when you forgive yourself. Being forgiven by God and by others is not enough. You must forgive yourself.

For most people, forgiving themselves is a challenge. They try, they struggle, and they fail. They just can't seem to get over it. In time, they grow accustomed to living in unforgiveness.

Not so with you! You are not an average person settling for an average existence! To get the peace you want and must have, forgive yourself.

Freedom #2 — Freedom from guilt

Do you feel guilty for something you did in the past? Before you answer that, do you know the difference between being guilty and feeling bad? If you are guilty of something, confess it, repent, make restitution if you need to, and move on. Once you've done all you can to make things right, you are done.

Guilt is supposed to drive you to get things right. Beyond that, feelings of "guilt" are just you feeling bad about what you did. Stop it! You don't need to be wasting your time feeling guilty. You dealt with it, so you are done.

> *"Forgiving others is the first step to forgiving ourselves."*
> *– Gerald G. Jampolasky, MD*

Feeling bad for something is different. Restitution can help, but if there is nothing you can do to right the wrong in your past, what are you going to do? Are you going to live like many do, with ulcers, sleepless nights, stomachaches, rashes, heart attacks, and more? You don't need to.

Come to grips with this reality: guilt is no longer the issue. You are free. If you still feel bad about it and can make amends, then do so. If you cannot fix it, then let it go. Forgive yourself.

Freedom #3— Freedom from the instant replay

The instant replay has been around a lot longer than sports on TV. Do you replay certain occurrences in your mind? We all do, but if you keep playing the same condemning film over and over, it begins to taint everything else you see and do. It hurts your attitude. It kills your creativity. It erodes your hopes and dreams.

You need to get rid of the film. Sure, what you did (as seen on the instant replay) was wrong, bad, and possibly even horrible, but does that mean you must play that film in your mind's eye for the rest of your life? Of course not!

Part of forgiving yourself involves mentally, emotionally, and spiritually throwing the old film away.

Freedom #4 — Freedom from self-punishment

For some reason, Christians are masters at self-punishment. We flog ourselves emotionally (and sometimes physically) over and over for what we've done. Why?

• **Because we think that eventually we will "pay off" the debt we feel we owe.** What nonsense! If your wrongs could be paid off through punishment, then who would need forgiveness?

• **Because we don't really think we have been forgiven.** Again, what nonsense! If others and God forgive us for what we have done, then we need to call it quits. What else can you do to make sure they have really forgiven you?

• **Because we think it's our duty to punish ourselves.** The self-punishment mindset has been around a long time. Somehow, the logic goes, we can extract a "pound of flesh" for our offense to balance out what we have done. But if you have been forgiven, what's the point in hurting yourself?

• **Because we can't forgive ourselves.** This is most likely the underlying reason behind all self-punishment. Naturally, if we cannot forgive ourselves, we will look for ways and reasons and opportunities to punish ourselves. It's a vicious cycle that will not stop ... until you forgive yourself!

Freedom #5 — Freedom to be confident and secure

If you cannot forgive yourself, then you are insecure and lacking in confidence. Put it this way — if you cannot forgive yourself, then you cannot accept forgiveness. Accepting forgiveness from others and from God is a prerequisite for forgiving yourself. And forgiving yourself is a prerequisite for confidence and security.

Sadly, if you cannot forgive yourself, you live with doubts. Your mind is filled with questions, like: *"Am I really forgiven? Are the people I hurt out to get me? Can I trust what they say? Am I okay with God? Is He going to bless me or curse me? Does He hear me? Why would He hear me, much less bless me, after what I've done?"*

From this negative mindset, it all goes downhill. But insecurity and lack of confidence can be replaced! You can trade them out for security and confidence. What joy! What freedom! The answer is in accepting forgiveness and forgiving yourself.

Freedom #6 — Freedom to feel worthy

Unforgiveness toward self is a downward spiral. At the bottom is the dirty dark sludge of worthlessness. It's thick, smelly, and almost impossible to wash off.

No doubt you know people who live at the bottom of the barrel of life. They conclude that it's their lot or their due punishment for what they have done. They accept the feelings of worthlessness and eventually the belief that they are worthless.

Nothing could be further from the truth!

Granted, you might have done something horrible, but you do not need to live at the bottom of the barrel of life. Get out of there! And to the sludge of worthlessness, say, *"I forgive myself!"* That is how you wash it off.

You are worthy of feeling worthy. Accept the forgiveness of others. Accept the forgiveness from God. And accept your own forgiveness. You can and you must. You are worth it!

Freedom #7 — Freedom to accept God's forgiveness

When you forgive yourself, you are free to genuinely and completely accept God's forgiveness. But the reverse is also true: if you cannot forgive yourself, it's impossible to truly accept God's forgiveness.

If you believe God has forgiven you, but struggle with forgiving yourself, then what is it you know that the Creator of the universe does not? Are you privy to some information that God is not? Perhaps you have found a truth or a line of reasoning that He has not yet discovered? Or maybe you think that what you've done is unforgivable?

The truth is, God cannot lie. When He says He forgives you, He forgives you.

Obviously, the perfect, holy, and all-knowing qualities of God trump any of our bits of logic, but why do we struggle with forgiving ourselves? Simple: because we just can't believe that God would forgive us!

The truth is, God cannot lie. When He says He forgives you, He forgives you. Psalm 103:12 states it boldly: *"As far as the east is from the west, so far has He removed our transgressions from us."* He forgives and He also removes. You can take that to the bank!

So, since He is God and you are not, you are free to forgive yourself. You are also free to accept God's forgiveness!

Freedom #8 — Freedom to NOT be perfect

Do you get upset with yourself when you are not perfect? Surely you don't think you are perfect, so then why is falling short of perfection such an issue?

You expect more from yourself; that's reasonable. You could have done better; that's probable. You should be perfect; that's not possible.

Unrealistic expectations have a way of seeping into the other areas of your life. Do you expect perfection from your spouse? From your children? From your employees? From your boss? From your friends?

And if so, the natural next step is to believe that acceptance and approval are based on perfection. Perfection first, then acceptance? Perfection first, then approval? It doesn't work that way!

> *"God does not give up on anyone, for God loved us from all eternity."*
> – *Desmond Tutu*

Such a view, belief, and approach will damage every relationship you have. People should accept you for who you are, and vice versa, but what about God? Does He expect perfection? No!

You do not need to be perfect before God will accept you or approve of you. He accepts you, period. He adopted you (Ephesians 1:5), He chose you (1:11), and He loved you and gave His Son for you (John 3:16) ... all before you were born, much less had a chance to show how perfect you were.

In short, you are free to forgive yourself for not being perfect. You cannot be perfect anyway, so quit stressing yourself out about not measuring up. Relax! You are approved and accepted by God. Reverend Edgell Franklin Pyles says, "In God's eyes, we are all broken and forgiven."

If God is okay with the fact that you aren't perfect, then you are certainly free to be imperfect.

Permission granted to forgive yourself

Do you need permission to forgive yourself? Perhaps you feel like you do. If that is the case, then read the following statements out loud:

From others: *"I receive forgiveness from others. I accept it."*

From God: *"I receive forgiveness from God. I accept it."*

From yourself: *"I receive forgiveness from myself. I accept it."*

> *You are free to accept forgiveness.*

If you accept forgiveness from others, then you have permission to forgive yourself. And if you accept forgiveness from God, then you certainly have permission to forgive yourself.

Unforgiveness is the cruelest punishment in the world. Give yourself the gift of forgiveness. Show yourself some love and forgive yourself. Matthew 22:39 commands you to *"love your neighbor as yourself."* Forgiving yourself is certainly an act of love.

You have permission to forgive yourself!

How to forgive yourself

All that remains is for you to do it, to actually go ahead and forgive yourself.

Here are the same 10 steps to forgiveness as they apply to forgiving yourself:

Step #1 — Decide on the hurt

Define what you did. What is it exactly that you want to forgive yourself for doing?

Step #2 — Be real, be honest

Don't add or remove anything from your incident. Make sure you are completely real and honest.

Step #3 — State what you want

Why do you want to forgive yourself? What is it you want? Be very clear with yourself.

Step #4 — Choose to forgive yourself

Choose. Make the decision that you are actually going to forgive yourself.

Step #5 — Verbalize your forgiveness

Begin with, *"I forgive myself for ..."* and complete the sentence, then add, *"And because I have forgiven myself, I am free!"* Stating what you are choosing to forgive yourself for is important, but what you want to repeat is the fact that you have forgiven yourself and that you are free!

Step #6 — Stop replaying the offense

Stop replaying the offense. Leave it alone. It's over. You put it to rest with forgiveness and don't need to bring it up any longer.

Step #7 — Show love

How do you show love to yourself? The same way you show love to those you forgive. You respect, honor, praise, encourage, believe in, and show kindness toward ... yourself.

Step #8 — Pray for yourself

Forgiving yourself is admittedly not an easy thing to do. Pray for yourself. Ask God for strength, wisdom, and help to rise above your situation to become a better person.

Step #9 — Look for reconciliation if possible

Reconciliation takes two people, but when you are forgiving yourself, it's a whole lot easier. It only takes you! Reconciling with yourself is about accepting—and being okay with—the fact that you are not perfect. Accept yourself as you are.

Step #10 — Move on

It's time to move on with your life. Leave what happened in the past. The list is gone (you burned it). You have forgiven yourself, so you are free to look at your future through the eyes of forgiveness. Move forward; move on.

> *Move forward; move on!*

Certain aspects of forgiving yourself might seem a little strange, but the whole process will make more sense as you do it. What matters is that you take the necessary steps toward forgiving yourself.

When that is done, you will be surprised at what you see, feel, and experience. Freedom is indeed a wonderful thing!

Putting forgiveness to work in my own life

The #1 distributor in one of my companies, Fred, was playing his own game. Unbeknownst to me, he was plagiarizing my programs. He was giving half of his time to his clone business and half of his time to selling for my business ... and he was still our #1 distributor!

He was an incredible salesman, but eventually it caught up with him. A customer from another state called me to say that he happened to have ordered my program and Fred's at the same time, only to find that they were identical.

It was news to me, so I called Fred. He was belligerent and unrepentant. He replied, "Well, that's life. That's business for you."

I filed a lawsuit, based on copyright infringement. In court, Fred was still his arrogant self. The judge was so insulted that she jailed him for two years and banned him from being in the self-improvement business for the rest of his life!

Though I never heard from him again after the court hearing, I had forgiven him before he ever went to jail. I was not going to let unforgiveness hold me down. When they closed his business, I bought all his plagiarized programs and burned them. I also bought his office furniture and gave it to charity or to friends.

Through forgiveness, I'm free. I hope Fred is.

CHAPTER SEVEN

Getting to the Source of Unforgiveness

Dig deep to be fully free!

Why is it to your benefit to go to the source and honestly deal with unforgiveness? Clearly, it is to set you free, but there is another reason for going deep. That reason is this: **Like everyone else in the world, you have the tendency to bury hurts.**

Additionally, the seeds of unforgiveness will grow no matter how deeply you bury them. A close friend of mine, John Bolten, recently told me an incredible story about unforgiveness.

Have you forgiven?

I visited a doctor in San Diego, California, several months ago. This doctor has treated over 15,000 terminally ill cancer patients. That's 15,000 individual cases! Almost all of them had been sent home to die by their own doctors, being given just months to live.

They came to this doctor with the desperate hope that he might be able to help them. The record shows that 54% of his patients have lived more than five years, and many have lived 10, 15, or more years. Some have died, but none of cancer.

I asked this doctor how he started a conversation with these patients, as many were depressed, some were angry at the world and at God, many were in great pain, and some were in wheelchairs, being too weak to walk. How do you start a conversation with such suffering, fear-ridden men, women, and children?

The doctor replied, "My first question is always the same—'**Have you forgiven?**'"

I was taken aback.

The doctor smiled, "The patients also give me a strange look and invariably ask, 'What does forgiveness have to do with my cancer?' I explain that we treat the complete individual. Man consists of body, soul, and spirit. If the soul or the spirit is sick, then the body is bound to be sick also."

That made sense.

The doctor said, "I'll ask them, 'Have you forgiven the friend that cheated you? Have you forgiven your spouse? Your children? Your parents, who may not even be alive? Did you have trouble with your siblings because of inheritance quarrels? Have you forgiven them? Have you forgiven yourself for some stupidity in the past? Think back, **have you forgiven?**'"

> *The time to forgive is always now.*

He continued, "You are only hurting yourself, even destroying yourself, if you have not forgiven. You are not hurting the other person, who may even be dead. If you have not forgiven, you are locked up in a cage. This cage is filled with hate, resentments, and feelings of revenge. There is only one door out of this cage. There is a big sign on this door that says: Forgive. Open this door. Step out. Then you can breathe fresh air again, and a tremendous burden will fall from your shoulders."

The time to forgive is NOW

I find it extremely interesting that forgiveness is the first thing this doctor discusses with his terminally ill patients. If anyone questioned the power of forgiveness, there is no question anymore! Remember the doctor's results: **54% of his patients lived more than five years, many lived 10, 15, or more years. Some have died, but none of cancer!**

In addition to showing the power of forgiveness, this story encourages me to do one thing: **deal with any unforgiveness in my life right NOW!** Why would anyone in their right mind let the seeds of unforgiveness grow unhindered? To quote the doctor, "Man consists of body, soul, and spirit. If the soul or the spirit is sick, then the body is bound to be sick also."

> *If the soul or the spirit is sick, then the body is bound to be sick also.*

The best preventative medicine is forgiveness. The moment you are hurt, choose to forgive right then. Don't let the unforgiveness take root in your life in any way, shape, or form. You know the steps to forgiveness. Start applying them as soon as the need arises.

Why forgiveness runs deep

Forgiveness runs deeper than unforgiveness. Remember that. No matter how much or how badly you have been hurt, it is possible to forgive and find healing.

What is sad is that most people will never get below the surface. They look at the outside issues. They focus on what they see or don't see and are not willing to pull away the layers and actually come to terms with what has been bothering them for so long.

Instead of finding the source and dealing with real issues, people stay shallow and, as a result, will only see unforgiveness. Forgiveness runs deeper, and it isn't until they choose to go deeper that they will find the answers they've been looking for.

Forgiveness runs deeper than unforgiveness because it *can* ... and because it *must*. That is good news for all of us!

Dealing with the root

Do you struggle with shame? Guilt? Condemnation? Hatred? Jealousy? Anger? Resentment? Insecurity? Instability? Whatever your battle, have you taken the time to get to the root cause?

Here's what is interesting: **At the bottom of every hurt, pain, and injustice lies the seeds of unforgiveness.** Dealing with the root cause of your battle will most likely reveal some unforgiveness that has grown in your heart, mind, and soul.

You must deal with it so you can move on. Author Colin C. Tipping notes, "Getting free of past bondages is vitally important." It doesn't matter what the bondage is; if you don't deal with it, you are still bound. As you know, the time to get rid of unforgiveness is now.

How fast can a boat travel with its anchor stuck in the mud? Silly question, but here's where it strikes closer to home:

- How loving can you be to your spouse when you still harbor unforgiveness in your heart?
- What do you expect from your relationship with your children if you are still at odds with your own parents?
- How far up the corporate ladder do you expect to get if you have suppressed your anger toward management?
- Do you trust God and still hold Him responsible for something bad that happened in your life?
- If you are single, how do you expect to find a confident and capable mate if you are insecure yourself?
- How financially stable do you plan to be if you are jealous of everyone who has something better than you?

Suppressed unforgiveness is especially dangerous because it has the ability to ruin your life—wholly, utterly, and completely! You can go from living the high life to living in the gutter.

It is so not worth it! Whatever the deep hurt, deal with it, and if unforgiveness has woven itself (and it probably has) into some area of your life, you know what to do with it!

Dealing with pain and denial

As you well know by now, pretending something did not happen is not forgiveness at all. It is denial in its purest form! Similarly, pretending that you have already forgiven yourself, God, or others is also denial.

> *The way to deal with real hurt and real pain is by being real, and the only way to be 100% real is to walk in forgiveness.*

Either way, denial is not an option because you have already chosen to forgive. The answer is to deal with issues as they come up. Face them head on. It might not be easy, and it most likely won't be comfortable, but it is necessary.

People typically deal with a hurt by burying it or blowing up about it. Admittedly, burying an issue will do more long-term damage than blowing up about it, **but neither approach will bring you the healing, wholeness, and freedom that you want and rightfully deserve**. The way to deal with real hurt and real pain is by being real, and the only way to be 100% real is to walk in forgiveness.

As you are walking in forgiveness, remember to filter everything through the definition of forgiveness. By doing that, you won't be fooled for a minute or get off track. You will know exactly what forgiveness is and is not. Keep these in the forefront of your mind:

Forgiveness IS:	**Forgiveness is NOT:**
✓ Acknowledging the hurt	✗ Approval
✓ Keeping your eyes open	✗ Forgetting
✓ Showing mercy	✗ Justifying
✓ Keeping no record of wrongs	✗ An obligation
✓ Living free from bitterness	✗ Giving in
✓ Taking responsibility	✗ Reconciliation
✓ Being honest about reality	✗ Re-hiring
✓ An attitude	✗ Trust
✓ A lifestyle	✗ Getting even

From this perspective, you can stand up for what is rightfully yours without feeling "bad" or thinking that you must "get even." Based on what you know forgiveness to be and not be, address every hurtful situation. Then choose to forgive and walk out that forgiveness.

That is how you both deal with the pain and remove denial from your vocabulary. Coming to terms with issues of unforgiveness will hurt. You are pulling a grown plant out by the roots and it's going to hurt! But it can be dealt with and it must be dealt with. You can do it!

Remember that healing begins the moment you choose to forgive.

Healing is coming your way

When you successfully deal with an issue of unforgiveness, you are stronger. You are better for it. And though it might not even be your intention, you have something to offer those who hurt you in the first place.

A friend of mine, a pastor, is a great example. After graduating from seminary, he went to pastor a small church in the South. The first several years went well and the little congregation grew. They completed work on the first building and started work on the second when something happened. Several people in the church started spreading lies about my friend. Everything ground to a halt. The deacon board leader, Wesley, spelled it out: "We want a different pastor."

Healing begins the moment you choose to forgive.

That was it. My friend and his wife packed their bags and left town. It hurt tremendously that the congregation had turned against them, but they chose to forgive. They moved to another city and started another life. About a year later, while on vacation in a nearby town, my friend happened to be passing through that same city. He stopped and chatted with a few acquaintances and learned that outspoken Wesley, the most affluent individual in the church, was now an alcoholic. What's more, he had lost his job and all of his assets, his wife divorced him, and his children disowned him.

Before my friend left town, he happened to see Wesley walking down the street. Here is what happened, in my friend's own words:

> I saw Wesley walking down the street, unkempt and dirty, I turned the car around and pulled up beside him. I rolled down the window and asked, "Do you know me?"
>
> Wesley looked at me through blurred, bloodshot eyes, blinked, and said, "Yes."

I asked, "Do you want me to help you?"

Wesley replied, "I sure do."

He got into the car and the smell of alcohol, sweat, and dirt was overpowering. We drove to the motel where he had been staying. They had kicked him out when he ran out of money and were holding his suitcase—a single suitcase containing all his remaining worldly possessions.

> *"Forgiving is very difficult most of the time, but people who have experienced the ecstacy of forgiveness find it easiest to forgive."* –*Steve Saint*

I paid the rest of his bill and put his suitcase in my car and drove him to a new motel where I checked him in, using my credit card. I took him to a doctor to get a vitamin shot, then back to the motel where I put him into the bathtub and gave him a bath. I spent the next few days getting him back on solid foods, bit by bit. I contacted his former wife and together we got him into the detox unit of the Veteran's Hospital.

I visited him several times before I left town. On one of my visits, Wesley was stone cold sober. Looking intently at me, he said, "You know I was one of the ones who opposed you."

"Yes," I said. "I know that."

"Then why?" he asked. "Why should you, of all people, do this for me?"

I replied, "I was able to love you when you didn't love me because God loved me when I didn't love Him. It's really that simple. I'm passing on what I received."

Months later, I received some great news: Wesley was still sober, he and his wife remarried, and he and the children reunited. He also got his job back. Only forgiveness can bring about such change.

Had my friend remained bitter and angry, he would have never picked Wesley up, much less even talked to him. But because of the healing that had taken place in my friend's heart, he was able to reach out and help one of the very people who had hurt him the most.

Healing not only affects you, it affects everyone around you!

Going deep takes time to recover

Like a scuba diver who must ascend slowly from the ocean depths, so it takes time to "resurface" after dealing with deep issues of unforgiveness. Don't put unrealistic expectations upon yourself to have everything back to normal. Not only is this unrealistic and unwise, but you don't want everything to be as it was. You have changed!

Take your time through the steps to forgiveness. You might feel raw, spent, or tired. You might even want to take a vacation. These feelings are natural and expected. After all, you have uprooted unforgiveness, which had its tentacle-like roots in every area of your life.

Repeat certain parts of the forgiveness process as necessary. Keep at it. You will win in the end!

Putting forgiveness to work in my own life

Charlie was a talented leader. People would follow him to the end of the world. He purchased one of my programs and went on to become one of our top salespeople.

I coached him and spent time with him each week for five years. I invested heavily in his personal growth and development as a leader because I knew he would accomplish great things.

The only problem was, he was simultaneously building his own company by stealing my people. That he would want to launch off on his own was fine. I've come to see that as a good thing and I wish them all success, but the fact that he wanted to take my people with him was something I could not allow.

I met with Charlie and told him point blank, "I've enjoyed helping you, but don't take any more of my people!" I was upset!

I was doing damage control and considering my options a week later when I heard the most unbelievable news: Charlie had died of a heart attack at age 43.

Though Charlie was gone, he had done considerable damage to another one of my companies. Honestly, it took me about six months to forgive him. Today, I am good friends with his family and grieve with them for their loss.

CHAPTER EIGHT

Forgiveness and Your Self-Image

Allow yourself to blossom!

I find it very interesting that those who know how to forgive also have a very positive self-image. This is no accident. Forgiveness is reflected in our self-image and our self-image is impacted by our ability to forgive. They are intrinsically connected.

Steve, a young man in Georgia, sent me his touching story.

Nobody wants me

From my earliest memory, nobody has wanted me. My parents divorced when I was only two years old. My father was a violent alcoholic. Unable to take care of a toddler and work (my mother received no child support), my mother sent me to live with her sister and brother-in-law in Maryland until she could get her life stabilized. This "temporary" situation with my aunt and uncle lasted until I graduated from high school.

My mother visited me every year, but she didn't want to take me back to New York to live with her. I could not understand what I had done or what was wrong with me that my mother did not want me.

Also, my uncle and I did not get along. My aunt told me that he felt like he was raising someone else's kid, so I always felt he resented me. He was big and loud and I was afraid of him. Even though I tried, I could never seem to please him. Nothing I did seemed good enough. I received no affirmation, just criticism. My biggest fear was that I would come home from school one day to find my suitcase out on the front porch and I would have nowhere to go.

My aunt took me to services at a church for a few years, but I never became close to God. I viewed Him as distant and non-caring and I blamed Him for my situation. I thought He was harsh and demanding and that I could never be good enough to please Him, so I avoided God, prayer, and church entirely.

In my senior year of high school, I finally rebelled against my uncle's harshness and my expected punishment came to pass; he kicked me out of the house. I was forced to leave all of my friends and go live with the woman who had rejected me and who was virtually unknown to me. I stayed with my mother for a year and then enlisted in the Air Force. I figured I would reject her like she had rejected me for all those years.

Unfortunately, the rejection I lived with my entire life left gaping holes in my heart. I tried to fill the holes with drugs, parties, and alcohol. After a brief stint in the Air Force, I moved to Hollywood to become famous. There, I sang in night clubs, entertained on cruise ships, and performed in professional theater groups, but fame eluded me. My appetite for alcohol and drugs, however, increased dramatically. I was fired from several jobs for stealing money to support my habit.

I even experimented with new age religions like Self Realization, Transcendental Meditation, and Astrology. I knew I was running away from the God of the Bible, but I was so angry with God that I gave up on Him and became an Agnostic. After four years, I left Hollywood. I was burned out and still not very famous.

I moved to New York, then to Atlanta. I hoped I could leave my problems behind, but they followed me. I was becoming a flat-out alcoholic like my father! Thankfully, out of 125 people I worked with, one lady noticed I was hurting and said something about Jesus being able to ease my pain.

"If God does exist," I replied, "then I know He is out to get me."

She wouldn't buy my rejection and explained how God loved me and wanted to forgive me.

"I'm not sure I want to forgive God," was my answer.

But through a series of events, I realized that God was real and that I must matter to Him. I was important. When that revelation hit, something inside me broke. **I asked Jesus into my heart.** I surrendered myself to Him and I felt God's love wash over me. At that moment, I knew that He forgave me and accepted me just as I was. He restored my self-confidence! Some months later, God totally delivered me from alcohol and drugs. I thank God that in 26 years I have never relapsed.

Because I knew God forgave me, it gave me the strength to forgive my father for abandoning me, my mother for rejecting me, and my uncle for making life so hard on me. I have been able to locate members of my father's family in Atlanta, and we now enjoy a family reunion each year. God restored our family and through His love and forgiveness, gave us the strength to forgive each other and ourselves.

Forgiveness and self-image go hand in hand

Almost without exception, people who do not forgive also have a negative self-image. There is a price to pay for being rejected, hurt, and abused, and our self-image bears the brunt of it.

The great news is that you can exchange a negative self-image for a positive one. Before I explain more about self-image and how to improve your positive self-image, it is important to again recognize the power of forgiveness.

> *Learning to forgive breeds an incredibly positive self-image.*

Those who learn how to forgive and practice forgiveness have an incredibly positive self-image. Something happens when they forgive that completely alters their self-image.

Here are several true examples of what happened to others when they chose to forgive:

Forgiveness makes you bold

With deliberate precision, the driver of a government truck turned his front bumper into the right rear wheel of the van, causing it to turn over three times sideways and once end over end. The police arrived and asked, "How many are dead?" Miraculously, only one of the five people needed hospital care. The target was Reverend Peter Dugulescu, pastor of First Baptist Church of Timisoara, Romania, and it was no accident. It was the fourth or fifth attempt on his life by the Romanian secret police.

Nine years later, after Pastor Peter was elected to Parliament in free Romania, he received a letter from his "appointed executioner," Jianu, who was in prison for five cold-blooded murders. Jianu had been a Communist executioner, and by his own confession, had killed others under order of the secret police. His letter stated with great detail his many attempts on Peter's life, including the road "accident" in Timisoara and an incident when the oxygen supply "ran out" while Peter was on the operating table and nearly died.

Jianu wanted to know one thing: *"Pastor Peter, will you forgive me? Can I still be forgiven? Please tell me, can you forgive me?"*

Peter investigated and found that Jianu was the most notorious and dangerous prisoner in the prison system. Could he be trusted? Was this a trap? Peter knew that Christ had died for just people like Jianu, so he chose to forgive.

Boldly, Peter visited the high security prison many times, taking Jianu food, Christian books, a cassette player, and sermon tapes. Over time, Jianu became a different person. He prayed and read his Bible, reading it from cover to cover every month. On November 5, 2000, Pastor Peter baptized Jianu inside the prison walls.

Forgiveness made Pastor Peter bold.

Forgiveness makes you strong

High school English teacher, Ray Payne, abducted and killed one of his 16-year-old students. The girl's mother, Betty Ferguson, was beside herself with rage. She cursed the killer on a daily basis and neglected her other children. She turned to alcohol to drown her sorrows. Consumed with hatred, she experienced severe backaches and headaches. To put it plainly, she was a mess.

Six years later at a funeral, Betty began to think about forgiveness. She read books on forgiveness and wondered if forgiving her daughter's killer would release her from her hate-filled prison.

After several months, praying, and working through forgiving the man who senselessly killed her daughter, Betty visited Ray in prison. She told him how much her daughter meant to her, how Ray had hurt her, and that she forgave him. They both cried.

"I left a different person," she said, and then added, "Forgiveness is the greatest gift I ever gave myself, and my children."

Betty now works in a Pennsylvania program for violent-crime victims as a mediator. Regarding her journey of forgiveness, she stated, "It has saved my life."

Forgiveness made Betty Ferguson strong.

Forgiveness allows you to do the impossible

Militant Hindus doused the car with gasoline and set it on fire. Trapped inside were Gladys Staines' husband and two sons, Philip, 10, and Timothy, 8. The attackers prevented their escape and kept rescuers away. The charred bodies were all that remained for Gladys and her remaining child, a daughter.

Gladys and her husband had been working with the lepers in India for many years, and this was their thanks! Instead of packing up and moving back home to Australia, Gladys and her daughter decided to stay and continue their work with the leprous outcasts. "We agreed that we would forgive those who did it," she explained. "And I can say from my own experience that forgiveness brings healing."

Since the killing in 1999, their work with the lepers has grown. Her act of forgiveness has had a massive impact on the community and outlying areas. People respect her and listen to her like never before.

Forgiveness allowed Gladys Staines to do the impossible.

Forgiveness makes others talk about you

A lawyer and a beautiful woman were engaged to be married. She broke it off for some reason, and he was furious. He planned retaliation. He paid a large sum of money for a hit man to go to her home, knock on the door, and throw acid in her face. As a result, she was blinded in one eye and considered legally blind in the other.

The lawyer and hit man were found guilty and sent to jail. Strange events followed. Two weeks after the lawyer was released from a several-year prison term, he married the woman he had blinded.

Reporters visited their house and asked the husband, "How can you live in the same home with the woman that you blinded?" The man answered, "Without her understanding and forgiving heart, I would not be here today. It is really only by the Grace of God."

The reporters then asked her, "How can you live with the man who blinded you?" She replied, "Life is too short to be bitter. I believe in forgiveness. The Lord taught us to forgive. I plan to do this the rest of my life … even if I am blind."

Forgiveness made others talk about this forgiving couple.

Forgiveness gives you strength to keep going

Gary was a new pastor at a church in Florida. One of the deacons, Jim, was a leader, a successful businessman, and possessed a lot of clout. Unfortunately for Gary, Jim was very unhappy with the way Gary was leading. He did everything possible to sway others away from Gary's plan. It got so bad that he would yell at Gary during business meetings.

Jim all but left the church. He refused to even look at Gary. Jim's life was miserable and even his friends distanced themselves from him. After about eight years of this, he scheduled a meeting with Gary.

When he walked into the church offices, he apologized to Gary for the things he had said and done! Both he and Gary cried and prayed together. In 15 minutes, everything had changed! Jim had newness of life. He was already a Christian, but this was a definite spiritual breakthrough. He looked different, acted different, and even walked differently.

For Gary, the eight-year walk of forgiveness was suddenly over. He had made it through. He was better for it, and Jim's life would never be the same.

Forgiveness gave Gary the strength to go on.

Forgiveness helps you mend broken relationships

Sally hated her spiteful mother and decided to move as far away from home as possible. She seldom went back, and when she did, she would spend the night with her brothers, never with her mother.

One day, Sally received a phone call that her mother was dying. Would she come? Did she even want to? Sally decided that she should at least visit her in the hospital. Her mother was indeed dying. She had no more than a few days left.

That night at the hospital, Sally couldn't sleep. She went to her mother's bedside and found her awake. Mustering all her courage, Sally said, "I'm sorry."

Her mom replied, "Me too."

With that, the wall of unforgiveness broke. The silence and coldness evaporated. They talked, laughed, and for the first time in decades, they said that they loved each other.

Later that very night, Sally's mother died. The wall of unforgiveness had come down. Thankfully, it wasn't too late!

Forgiveness helped mend Sally's broken relationship.

Forgiveness enables you to show mercy

During one of the persecutions of the Armenians by the Turks, an Armenian girl and her brother were pursued by a Turkish soldier. He trapped them at the end of a lane and killed the brother before the sister's eyes. The sister managed to escape by leaping over a wall. She fled the country and became a nurse.

Several years later, a wounded soldier was brought to her hospital. She recognized him at once as the soldier who had killed her brother and had tried to kill her. His condition was such that the least neglect or carelessness would result in his death.

The nurse gave the soldier the most painstaking and constant care. One day, while on the road to recovery, the sick man recognized her as the girl whose brother he had slain.

He said to her: "Why have you done this for me as I was the one who killed your brother?"

"I am a Christian and the Bible teaches us to forgive," she replied.

Forgiveness enabled the Armenian nurse to show mercy.

Forgiveness changes everything!

Clearly, forgiveness changes everything! It energizes, empowers, and literally changes your life! It does this in part by its effect on your self-image. How can people who have been through so much hurt and pain show such incredible boldness, strength, love, hope, and mercy if their self-image has not changed?

As you know, one absolutely essential ingredient for success in any endeavor, no matter how big or how small, is that of a positive self-image. That is because the world operates on the basis of the law of attraction: **what you are and what you think will attract corresponding conditions**.

> *The secret is to form positive self-image habits!*

If your self-image is positive, you attract positive results, but if you have a negative self-image, you attract negative results. This may appear simplistic, but it is absolutely true!

With forgiveness, it works like this: Let's say you have a backstabbing workmate who loves to criticize you at the office. If your attitude is, *"No matter what happens, I choose to forgive,"* then you will be surprised how resilient and strong you will be. The verbal attacks will bounce off you like a ball against a wall. Your attitude of forgiveness will attract to itself a strength, an impenetrableness, that will not be denied.

On the other hand, if you go to work still upset at the last lie your workmate told about you, you are asking for trouble. You will be the target of as much abuse as possible ... because you were looking for it. You attracted it to yourself.

What is your self-image?

Your self-image is your mental picture of yourself and is made up of what you believe about your potential, talents, abilities, and worth as a person. This mental picture determines the measure of confidence you bring to everything you say, think, and do.

But your self-image is more like a movie than a single picture. Day by day and frame by frame, your experiences, what other people say and do, and how you respond to all of these occurrences, compound to affect your self-image.

Over time, habits form. Your subconscious mind then tells you that this is the type of person you are. The secret is to form positive self-image habits!

You can change your self-image!

Your self-image or mental picture is based on what you believe and the habits you form on a daily basis. In short, your self-image is the result of choices you make.

Some believe in fate or that our choices are simply the result of past conditioning, but I believe that we always have control over our choices. Past conditioning affects you, but choices are here and now. They are new.

Honestly, knowing that I can control my future by making my own choices motivates me, excites me, and gives me hope for a better tomorrow!

You change your self-image (into one that is a more accurate picture of your real, God-given potential) the same way you built your present self-image: by daily exercising your power of choice!

Remain a perfect "10"

One of the most important elements in building a powerful self-image is what I call the I/R Theory. It is simple but not simplistic, and it has the power to change your life! I'll explain the I/R Theory, and then show how it directly relates to forgiveness.

Let's begin with the score. Being a perfect "10" is not about good looks. It's about being you. The "I" represents your Identity and the "R" represents your Role. On a scale of 1-10, with 10 being the best, see both your Identity and your Role as perfect 10s.

Now, suppose it's Monday and everything that can go wrong does go wrong: car accident, argument with loved one, missed job promotion, misbehaving child, rain, headache, broken garage door, etc. You name it, it's happening.

Never combine your identity with your role.

How do you feel at this point? Probably not a perfect "10," right? But remember, your "I" is your Identity and is ALWAYS a "10." You are always you. Your Identity is never in question ... but your Role (that of a driver, spouse, friend, teacher, parent, homeowner, etc.) can improve. There is room for growth. That is not something you should feel bad about! If you need to get better at something, then do it.

Pay attention here ... ***never let what happens to you in your Role affect who you are in your Identity.*** You might feel like a "3" in your Role as a parent, for example, but your Identity is always a "10."

Trouble comes when people see their Identity as a "3" as a result of their poor performance in their Role. Their self-image is crushed. They feel worthless, hopeless, and inferior.

Many ride the roller coaster of emotions, feeling great about themselves when they do well and then horrible about themselves when they perform poorly. This lifestyle breeds abuse (toward self and others), attitude problems, confusion, and more!

The secret is this: **Accept that your Identity is a perfect "10" and accept that your score for your Role is open for improvement.** Then move on!

When it comes to forgiveness, the same distinct categories apply. Author Lewis B. Smedes says it well: "Forgive what people do, not who they are." You cannot forgive a person for being that person, but you certainly can forgive them for what they do to you.

The power of this principle comes into play when you apply it to ***yourself***! You might have done something wrong (your Role), but it does not mean that you are a bad person (your Identity). Forgive yourself and move on. Peace, self-confidence, and rest come when you see that you are always a perfect "10."

Let that reality boost your self-image into the skies ... where it ought to be!

Believe in your unlimited potential

Everyone has an overall pattern of thinking that is generally either positive or negative. Naturally, the pattern you choose will profoundly affect your life!

Belief in your unlimited potential causes you to take the necessary action for success. But believing the opposite will cause you to doubt your ability to achieve.

Belief in your unlimited potential causes you to see challenges as opportunities for growth, advancement, and success. Believing the opposite is to see challenges as threats and impossibilities.

Belief in your unlimited potential causes you to confidently say, "*I can!*" and "*I will!*" Believing the opposite is to reactively say, "*I can't*" or "*I doubt.*"

My chosen belief is that I can do anything. I wake up each day without giving mental recognition to the possibility of defeat. This is my attitude and it affects everything I do, say, or think.

Allow this belief to spill over into your ability to forgive. Boldly declare, "*I will forgive others no matter what they do to me!*" When that is your belief, you are freed even more to reach your unlimited potential.

How to increase YOUR belief in your unlimited potential

Strengthening your positive self-image is worth every ounce of effort because the payoff is incredible! Forgiveness is certainly not easy at times, but it, too, is worth every ounce of effort.

The following four-step plan will help strengthen your positive self-image:

Step #1 — Learn the power of dreams.

A goal begins as a dream, and unless you can imagine something new, you have nowhere to go except where you have been. Look up! Expand your horizons! Discover a dream that is so important that you are willing to commit your life to it.

Your dream will bring focus like never before.

Dreams give you the ability to see the possible, visualize it as the probable, and transform it into reality. Your dream will bring focus like never before.

Step #2 — Cultivate a burning desire to reach your dreams.

Desire spells the difference between mere daydreams and goals. Desire kindles motivation, builds enthusiasm, sparks creativity, and triggers action.

Desire can be cultivated by keeping your purpose and goals before you daily. Review the benefits of achieving them and desire will burn within you.

Step #3 — Exercise your freedom of choice.

Act on your freedom to choose or you will lose that freedom. If you hesitate, others will choose for you and tell you what to do, directing you toward their goals, not yours.

Use your freedom of choice to design a stronger, more positive self-image for yourself. If you are fearful, choose courage. If you are timid, choose to love people. If you frequently procrastinate, choose to take action now. If you have always waited for others to lead, choose to act on your own initiative now.

Step #4 — Learn who you are.

Learning who you are includes learning what your Creator says you can do. Scripture says, *"I can do everything through Him who gives me strength"* (Philippians 4:13). Knowing who you are and what you can do will forever change your self-image!

> *Only we can limit ourselves.*

God places no limits on us and nobody else has the power or authority to limit us. Only we can limit ourselves.

Forgive! Don't let unforgiveness limit you in any way. Be free, just as God intended you to be!

Putting forgiveness to work in my own life

Frank, who ran a leasing business in Colorado, knew how to bring decision-makers together. He and his banker met with me and several other Colorado businessmen with his plan. The result would be a 15% return paid quarterly.

We all studied his numbers, asked questions, and invested. I'm still out more than two million dollars! I'll never see a penny of it. Frank was and is a scammer. He bilked money out of people who needed it to survive, but he doesn't care. I forgive him and pray for him. Someday he'll pay for what he's doing.

CHAPTER NINE

How to Receive Forgiveness

Another absolute must!

Learning how to ***receive*** forgiveness, now that is much different than learning how to give forgiveness! This true story of a man in Oklahoma is a great example of receiving forgiveness.

Grateful to receive forgiveness!

As an engineer, I would occasionally travel and do consultant work in other states. On one of these trips, I met Judy. She worked for a company that we did work with, so our paths would cross about every six months. It wasn't my intent to have an affair and cheat on my wife and two children, but it just happened.

The obvious plan was to keep it a secret, but Judy called the home as a "business call" to see if I would be traveling again soon. My wife became suspicious and grilled me. I denied it for days, but she finally broke me down and I told her the truth.

At that point, my wife went ballistic! She was angrier than a volcano is hot, and I'm not exaggerating! The children knew Mom was mad at me, but we didn't tell them the whole story.

We visited with our pastor who suggested we get some marriage counseling. That hurt my pride, needing to go to a counselor, but my wife wanted to go and I knew I'd pay for it if I didn't go.

The first few sessions were nothing but my wife saying how much of a lousy cheat I was. I apologized about 20 times, but that didn't seem to penetrate her thick head. She wasn't hearing me. "How many times do you want me to apologize and say I'm sorry?" I asked her.

Her reply was always the same, "I want you to feel the pain that you have caused me."

She was hurt, and I could understand why, but her rage hadn't subsided one bit in 60 days. What hurt the most was that she would look at the counselor and say, "He's just lucky I haven't taken the kids and divorced him."

The counselor then asked her a question that stopped her cold: "How much is enough? How much hurt do you need to give him to satisfy your rage?"

While my wife sat there, thinking up a reply, I asked, "Why can't she just forgive and forget?"

The counselor's look put me in my place. "You are asking the impossible when you ask her to forgive and forget," he explained. "The real struggle in your betrayal of your marriage vows is that she has to forgive and REMEMBER. The memory never goes away."

I was beginning to understand just how deeply I had hurt my wife and how my trite apologies were worthless. Could she ever forgive me? Would she? I decided right then that I would never ask her again to forget. Being forgiven for what I did would be enough, more than enough.

As I was thinking, my wife spoke up, "I think I have had enough. I am ready to forgive."

The counselor explained, "Forgiveness is a point in time as well as a process. Forgiveness begins with the willingness to say I am sorry, but it is a process that will be worked out over time as you rebuild your relationship."

We looked at each other and agreed that we wanted to begin the process of forgiveness. For the first time in months, we held hands. I looked in her eyes and said, "I am so sorry. Can you ever forgive me?"

I was crying at that point, and so was she. She nodded her head and said, "Yes, and I'm sorry too."

Then she said the three most meaningful words I have ever heard: "I love you." How she could love me at this point was beyond me. She forgave me, and I knew it. It felt incredible to be forgiven! We went to counseling for several more months as we worked to repair and improve our marriage. Forgiveness is indeed a process and a choice.

Today, our children are all grown and our marriage is deeper and closer than ever before. I will forever be grateful to my wife for the forgiveness she gave to me.

You can *give* forgiveness, but can you *receive* it?

Most of what we have learned and discussed to this point has been about forgiving others, forgiving God, and forgiving yourself. Forgiveness is obviously a necessary skill, but it includes ***both*** the giving and receiving of forgiveness.

Have you mastered the art of receiving forgiveness? Do you know how to ask for and receive forgiveness?

To best understand how to receive forgiveness, it is important to know what you are asking. **You are asking the person you hurt to:**

- Acknowledge the hurt
- Show you mercy
- Keep no record of wrongs
- Take responsibility
- Keep his/her eyes open
- Not be bitter toward you
- Be honest about reality
- Maintain a forgiving attitude

You are asking a lot! It is valuable to recognize that. In addition, keep in mind that **you are NOT asking the person you hurt to:**

- Approve of what you did
- Forget what you did
- Justify what you did
- Be obligated to forgive you
- Give in to you
- Reconcile with you
- Re-hire you
- Trust you
- Get even with you

You want to be forgiven. That is the whole reason behind asking for forgiveness, not to mention wanting to clear your conscience, get your peace back, and possibly restore the broken relationship. Forgiveness is good, whether you give it or receive it, but recognize that asking for forgiveness is not a flippant gesture. You are asking, not demanding.

With that in mind, how do you practically go about asking for and receiving forgiveness? Here is how:

To Receive Forgiveness
#1 — acknowledge what you have done

Did you hurt someone? What did you do, specifically? Have you acknowledged what you've done?

First, acknowledge **to yourself** that you indeed did what you did. You are not playing games. You are taking complete responsibility for your actions.

> *Having regret has nothing to do with asking for forgiveness.*

Second, acknowledge what you did **to the person** you hurt. This is obviously the hard part. Be real, be honest, and be humble. Also, be very specific and clear.

Let's say (since this is something that we should be learning and teaching at a young age) you hit a ball that broke your neighbor's window. You would need to go to his house and tell him, "*I broke your window with my ball.*"

To Receive Forgiveness
#2 — apologize

After you acknowledge what you have done, it is time to apologize. Say you are sorry for whatever you did. "*I'm sorry for breaking your window,*" you might say.

This is not a time to say you "regret" doing what you did. Of course you regret doing it. You got caught! You are guilty. The CEO regrets that he sank the business that employed you, especially if he has to pay for it. The drunk driver regrets that he killed your child, especially if he goes to jail because of it. The cheating wife regrets that she hurt her husband, especially if she loses the children because of it.

Having regret has nothing to do with asking for forgiveness. Regret is not an apology. It is nothing more than a trite, politically correct way to say, *"I'm sorry I got caught."*

Instead, your apology should be a real apology where you take responsibility for your actions and say you are sorry for what you did. No hedging or hiding. You honestly deal with it.

To Receive Forgiveness
#3 — ask for forgiveness

The next step is to ask for forgiveness. You have acknowledged your actions and apologized for what you did. Now, boldly ask for forgiveness. You want to clear the air and make things right.

> *The act of asking for forgiveness is not easy, nor should it be.*

Going back to the example of the ball through the window, saying *"Please forgive me for breaking your window,"* might seem a bit odd since nobody got hurt, but asking for forgiveness is based on what you did, not on someone else's pain level or degree of discomfort. The neighbor who owns the window is impacted because now he has to pay for replacing the window. There is a cost involved, even though nobody was hurt.

Asking for forgiveness is one of the hardest things to do in life— ***and it should be!*** The blow to your ego caused by humbling yourself and asking for forgiveness is usually nothing compared to what you did.

The fact that asking for forgiveness is hard is the very reason that most people won't do it. It hurts, so they choose to ignore it, forget it, or bring it out into the open but not take direct responsibility for it. The only way to get the forgiveness you want is to actually ask for it!

Remember, you want forgiveness, and even expect it, but ***you cannot demand it.*** You are sincerely asking to be forgiven, but it's not a guarantee.

If, on the odd chance, the person refuses to forgive you for whatever it is you have done, remember: **forgiveness requires only one person, while restoration requires two people**. You can still walk free of an issue (and forgive yourself!) even if the person you apologize to refuses to forgive you.

The truth is that if this happens, the person you are talking to needs a ***lot*** more help than you do. You are free; you have done your part, but he or she remains shackled by the chains of bitterness and unforgiveness. *(If this ever happens to you, give the person this book. Seriously! Then email me a note and I'll send you another book at no charge.)*

To Receive Forgiveness
#4 — make amends

The broken window needs to be replaced ... ***by you.*** That is what taking responsibility is all about. After you have stated your actions, said you were sorry, and asked for forgiveness, the immediate next step is to make amends. *"Let me know how much it costs to fix it and I'll repay you,"* you might say. Or, if you do not have the money, you can be creative: *"I'll mow your yard as many times as it takes to cover the cost of the window."*

Whatever it takes to fix what you broke and make restitution, it is your responsibility to do so. A great example is tax collector Zacchaeus in the Bible. He said to those he had been ripping off, *"If I have taken anything from anyone by false accusation, I restore fourfold"* (Luke 19:8).

As a tax collector, Zacchaeus was hated, despised, and feared. Imagine the difference when he offered to return what he had unrightfully taken ... multiplied by four! That is taking restitution seriously. And don't you think that people would gladly forgive him if he were apologizing AND offering quadruple reimbursement? Of course!

Making restitution is what making amends is all about. Honestly, you would expect nothing less from someone asking for your forgiveness.

What can you do if what you did cannot be fixed? Someone killed, innocence taken away, memories, loss, and more. Some things can never be put back together, ***but you can still ask for forgiveness!***

Most people do not know how to receive forgiveness.

Forgiveness is all about being forgiven for what you cannot fix, repair, or replace. That is precisely why forgiveness costs the person doing the forgiving. As the recipient of forgiveness, you must understand that the person forgiving you is paying a price. Understand that very clearly. This is another reason why asking for forgiveness is serious business.

So, if you cannot fix, repair, or replace what it is you are asking forgiveness for, what you want is mercy. You rightly deserve punishment of some sort for the hurt, damage, or pain that you caused, but mercy is wiping it away—not claiming it never happened, but not making you pay for it.

When asking for forgiveness, your job is to make amends and, if necessary, ask for mercy. Giving forgiveness and showing mercy are entirely up to the other person.

To Receive Forgiveness
#5 — actually receive it

When you have acknowledged specifically what you've done, apologized, asked for forgiveness, and made amends (even if the making amends part lasts for a long while, that is fine), the last and final step is to ***receive*** the forgiveness you are requesting.

To really receive forgiveness, and not just go through the motions, you need to be willing to do several things:

- Will you let it go?
- Will you NOT let what you've done in your past affect your future?
- Will you lay down the burden of guilt?
- Will you forgive yourself?
- Will you trust that the price has been paid?
- Will you allow yourself to be free?

Sadly, most people are not good at actually receiving forgiveness. For some reason, they cannot or will not let go of what they did. It makes me wonder, ***what's the point in asking for forgiveness if you aren't willing to receive it?***

You can, should, and MUST receive forgiveness! Only then will you be able to experience the wonderful freedom that forgiveness brings.

Receive forgiveness ... so you can forgive

Sometimes, accepting forgiveness frees us up to forgive ourselves, others, and God. Tom is a great example. He grew up poor in a metropolitan city. It was tough socially, physically, and emotionally. His father ran the family into debt and then left when Tom was just starting high school. His mother was depressed and continually told him that he was unloved and unwanted.

Two of his friends invited him to a local church youth group. There, Tom found hope in a relationship with Jesus Christ. "For the first time in my life, I understood the love that God had for me," Tom explained. "What I learned about God and the friends He gave me brought me out of my depression and gave me great hope for my family."

Sadly, a few years later, Tom's mother committed suicide. He was angry and hurt, but he recognized that God was not to blame. He states, "Through forgiveness toward my mother, father, and others, I learned that I didn't need to forgive God, **but I needed to receive His forgiveness so that I could forgive myself and then others.**"

Now, Tom has a restored relationship with his father and speaks to him regularly on the phone. "I count the blessings that God has given to me because of forgiveness," Tom now states. Quite a change from hating his father!

If you cannot forgive, how can you be forgiven ... and if you cannot be forgiven, how can you forgive? Giving and receiving forgiveness go hand in hand.

Putting forgiveness to work in my own life

I have businesses in many countries. Several years ago, I received an urgent call from one of my international company presidents, saying, "We've had a mutiny! Jon came to the office today and at gunpoint kicked everyone out!"

Jon, one of my trusted leaders, had stolen our office, our equipment, our products, and many of our clients. His staff occupied our building and maintained business as usual. The only thing Jon did not have were the salespeople that I had hired.

What's more, I knew the legal system in this foreign country was slow and that it would take years before we saw any justice. Jon knew this as well, so I had to do something else, and fast!

I immediately flew in and met with my staff and salespeople to plan. Somehow, Jon remained one step ahead of us, so we also figured out that there was a mole on our sales team.

At this point, I immediately cancelled all existing contracts and scheduled a meeting with the entire sales force. I stood up and explained, "We have a mole among us. I am a master at reading body language and can tell who in here is that mole." In a matter of minutes,

I picked the man out. He was 25 rows back, 4 seats in. We pulled him out of the meeting and he confessed.

The mole gave us the names of the top 10 people who worked for Jon. Then, at 8 a.m. the next morning, we simultaneously raided the 10 residences of these individuals (we had a sheriff and an attorney with us at each house) and demanded inventory back. We got 90% of our products back this way.

As expected, it took years and multiple lawsuits before justice was served. Our new business grew and proved to be highly successful, even with the 25% loss of revenue (thanks to Jon's mutiny). Eventually, we won all the lawsuits, but it took several years. Jon never admitted his error, much less made amends, but I chose to forgive him. I still pray for Jon and his family. Perhaps one day Jon will ask for forgiveness. I would gladly accept his apology.

CHAPTER TEN

Let Forgiveness Set You Free!

Time to fly!

When all is said and done, forgiveness sets you free. That is, I believe, what forgiveness is all about. The following story about a man who lives across town from his ex-wife and daughter is an incredible example of the freedom that forgiveness can bring ... if forgiveness is allowed.

Free from consuming hatred

One morning, on the 6 a.m. news, I saw that there was a fire on the block where I had lived ... and it was my house! My wife and I were separated, and she lived there with our daughter. When I arrived, the neighbors told me they had taken my daughter to one hospital and my wife to a burn unit at another hospital. My daughter survived, but my wife was so badly burned that she died two days later.

My wife's boyfriend was staying with them when the fire started. His story was, "She poured a can of gasoline on herself and set herself on fire."

I knew in my heart that this was not the case, but the police had no evidence that said otherwise. After the funeral, the case was closed. I knew then that it was up to me to get revenge. I thought, planned, and dreamed of how I would kill my wife's boyfriend.

For 11 years, I didn't think of anything else. One night I took a gun and went looking for him. Thankfully, I never found him, because if I had, I would have killed him and then fought to the death with the police.

To say the least, my hatred consumed me. It ruined my life. I was so focused on getting even that I neglected everything, including my daughter. I believed that life was not worth living. I was drinking everyday and tried to commit suicide several times. Once, I overdosed on pills, but someone found me and took me to a hospital, and another time I tied heavy objects to my legs and jumped into the Baltimore harbor, but people on a boat saw me and pulled me out. I ended up spending a lot of time in mental wards.

It was a never-ending nightmare. I happened to meet two men who took interest in me and challenged me to pray for and forgive the very person who had caused me so much grief. "These guys are crazy!" I thought to myself.

Over a period of time, however, I found that they were right. I prayed and asked Jesus to forgive me for my sins. It was a new beginning for me. I knew in my heart that the next step was to forgive. I started by praying for my wife's boyfriend, then saying that I forgave him. A calm peaceful feeling came over me!

Today, I am not bound by hatred or anger. I am free!

Forgiveness sets you free to enjoy life!

Though forgiveness will set you free, it is important that you move from a generality to a specific in order to see exactly how forgiveness can set you free.

Free to Enjoy: Purpose

Sometimes, unforgiveness can get us so messed up that we get off track, losing sight of our gifts, our calling, and our purpose. When we walk in forgiveness, we are able to reach our full potential.

Alejandro Lopez is a great example. He grew up in Honduras in a disintegrated home under his grandfather and mother's authority. Raised traditionally as Roman-Catholic, Alejandro says, "I met the Lord as my personal Savior at age 15, but my 'friends' pushed me to drink with them."

> *"Though unforgiveness can eat at you like a cancer, forgiveness can set things right or even make things better."*
> *– Jim Gray*

Alejandro became an alcoholic and quit school. Soon after, he got married. Three children later, his wife died suddenly and he was left alone. Still an alcoholic, Alejandro was fired from every job he had. Somehow, he managed to start a business that proved profitable, but he could not keep his life in order. His growing business sank with him. When the banks and suppliers sued him, Alejandro found himself in jail.

He was surrounded by murderers, killers, gang members, drug dealers, and kidnappers. He witnessed rapes, assassinations, fights, pain, starvation, lack of hygiene, and overcrowded cells; Alejandro was at rock bottom. And to top it off, the lawyer he paid to get him out of jail simply pocketed the money.

Alejandro prayed, "God, please get me out of here! Why am I here?"

In the darkness, he says, "I felt God tell me, 'Your mission is to work for Me in this very place.'"

Alejandro couldn't believe his ears, but he was faithful. He prayed for strength and told others about God's love. The number of converts grew from two to over 1,000 and it became the first prison church officially recognized by the Honduran Government.

It was not an easy journey, but Alejandro explains, "God taught me to forgive and not hold it against people and to remember the bitterness without pain or regret. I was physically in prison, but I was spiritually free!"

Unexpectedly, after eight years in jail, Alejandro received a letter from the judge telling him that there was not enough evidence for his imprisonment and that he was free to go! Alejandro appeared before the judge and the judge apologized, to which Alejandro replied, "I forgive you and the courts for the injustice done to me."

Then Alejandro went and registered his prison church with a local Pastor's Association. Today, he preaches on Radio and TV programs and in different churches and prisons around Honduras. He is also the pastor of the church he founded in prison. In addition, he counsels the prisoners and helps provide skill training, computer courses, and work for some inmates when they are released from jail.

Alejandro is an example of freedom that only forgiveness can bring.

Free to Enjoy: Answers

Not every situation is black and white. Sometimes there are complexities that require you to walk, step by step, from choosing to forgive to finding the answers you need.

Rob found that to be the case in a very real way. Early one Saturday morning, he drove to his pastor's house and banged on the door. "What's going on?" asked the pastor as he opened the door.

Rob stammered, "Sally is pregnant, but I'm not the father!"

When all is said and done, forgiveness sets you free.

It was a bombshell, to say the least! Rob was angry, and rightfully so, but what should he do? He asked his pastor, "What do I do about Sally? Do I forgive her? I want to kick her sorry butt out of the house and divorce her! I can't believe she did this! It's affected everything: her work, her life, my work, my life, and our future. She's ruined everything!"

What Rob said was true; Sally had done a great job single-handedly sinking their ship. Adultery has a way of shaking every foundation. What should he do? Rob needed answers, and needed them fast.

The pastor advised, "Knowing right from wrong in this situation is obviously not the issue. The real question is whether you will forgive her or not."

Rob nodded. "I know, but even if I wanted to, I'm not sure I could forgive her."

They talked about forgiveness, about love, and about Sally's adultery. They talked about how to forgive and the fact that, as Christians, we have been forgiven for all of our sins. They talked about being forgiven and what that means. And they prayed.

The more they talked, the more Rob seemed in control. "No doubt the forgiveness process will take time," he stated, "but I'm willing to do it." Then he said, "I'm not justifying what Sally did, but I'm not going to hold it over her. I forgive her and choose to love this child as if it were my own."

The moment he said he was going to love the child as his own, Rob had the answers he was looking for. It began with choosing to forgive, and from there it snowballed.

When the baby girl arrived, Rob was beside himself with joy. He sent out hundreds of pink cards and chocolate. You would have never known it was not his child ... and he would never tell. That was an agreement he and Sally had made together.

The beautiful little baby girl turned out to be the love of Rob's life! He delighted in her and, as promised, raised her as his own. Sally could not have asked for a more loving husband and father to her child. The little girl blossomed into a beautiful woman, loved, accepted, and confident. She went on to have a successful career, never knowing that it all began with forgiveness.

Whatever your situation, when you choose to forgive, you will find the answers you need.

Free to Enjoy: Clarity

Life can be confusing at times, especially when people are purposefully playing with your mind.

When Steve was young, he innocently believed that his family was perfect. He had no idea that his father, a pastor, was drifting away, becoming more and more consumed by pornography, alcohol, and illegal financial activity. His parents divorced soon after.

Eventually, everything came into the light and Steve was both heartbroken and confused. At the age of 14, Steve's father began to pelt him with questions, like: "Why did you stay with your mom? Don't you love me anymore? Why won't you live with me? Do you think I'm a criminal? Don't you know that your mom is brainwashing you?"

Steve began to hate his father. "I was consumed by thoughts of him dying, as if that were the only way I could be healed inside," Steve admits. "I wanted to rip him apart for everything he had done to hurt our family."

You must state exactly what it is you are choosing to forgive.

Years later, when Steve was in college, something happened. Steve explains, "I felt like I hit a brick wall spiritually. I asked God why I was feeling this way, but I knew all along what it was. I knew I had to forgive my dad, but I refused. I resisted. I wouldn't do it. My grades slipped lower and lower, relationships turned sour, and financially I was in trouble. I fell into a deep depression and ended up taking medication for an ulcer. Finally, I told God that He had won. I would forgive my dad."

Steve drove eight hours to have breakfast with his father. Right there in the restaurant, Steve apologized for hating him and for holding things against him for so long. Steve says, "I told him that although I did not approve of his life or condone the things that he had done to me, I forgave him and loved him because God loved him."

The result?

Steve happily states, "The freedom and healing that was released because I forgave has transformed my life! Everything that I lost because of my hate has been restored to me."

The good thing about forgiveness is that it requires that you begin with the problem. There is no ambiguity. You must state exactly what it is you are choosing to forgive. In so doing, you are clarifying the hurt (what happened) and your goal (to forgive). From there, you find freedom.

Free to Enjoy: Peace, kindness, and gentleness

A friend of mine, Chuck, from Dallas, Texas, was a great Christian man who told me point-blank, "I can't forgive a certain person who has hurt me so deeply. I've tried many times to forgive, but I just can't turn it loose."

I made him an offer: "I'll mail you articles and quotes and material on forgiveness, once a week, for a year, if you will read it all."

He agreed to read what I would send him. Less than six months later he called me and said, "You don't need to send me anything else about forgiveness. It worked."

We both cried and prayed over the phone. It was a great day! From that moment forward, he was a kinder, gentler, more peaceful man. Forgiveness totally changed his life!

Free to Enjoy: God's mercy

When someone forgives you and you are not required to repay what you owe, you experience mercy. It is a wonderful thing to be given mercy by those we have hurt, whether the hurt was intentional or unintentional. Mercy is given to us. We cannot earn it, buy it, or beg for it. Mercy is wholly and completely undeserved.

> *"The forgiven life is the forgiving life."*
> – *Jim Gray*

Forgiveness also frees you to enjoy the biggest act of mercy of all time: God's mercy!

When Psalm 103:10 says that God *"does not treat us as our sins deserve or repay us according to our iniquities,"* what it is saying is that God is giving us mercy. After all, scripture makes it plain:

- that the *"wages of sin is death"* (Romans 6:23),
- that *"all have sinned and fall short of the glory of God"* (Romans 3:23), and
- that *"your iniquities have separated you from God"* (Isaiah 59:2).

Without question, we all make mistakes and need forgiveness. We all have sinned, and for our sins, we owe. The penalty is death. In the midst of this, we must ask: **Why would God extend mercy?** The answer is exhilaratingly powerful: ***Because He loves us more than any of us can imagine!***

But since our sins separate us from God, **how could the relationship between God and man be restored?** There is only one answer: ***Through a sacrifice big enough to cover all sin (past, present, and future sin) for all mankind.***

This leaves us with one last question: **What type of sacrifice could cover all sin for all people for all time?** For that, there is again only one answer: ***God's Son, Jesus Christ***

That is the biggest act of mercy of all time! God did it for you. It's yours, free to enjoy, if you will accept it.

Free to Enjoy: God's forgiveness

Forgiveness is a journey, one that leads each one of us to the same pivotal spot: ***the cross of Jesus Christ.*** You can learn to forgive others and learn to receive their forgiveness, but there is more to the picture. The journey of forgiveness is only complete when you experience God's forgiveness.

To experience the forgiveness of God and to accept His mercy means that you receive His forgiveness. As you well know by now, to receive forgiveness, you must:

- acknowledge what you have done,
- apologize,
- ask for forgiveness,
- make amends, and
- actually receive it.

With God, acknowledging that you have sinned is pretty easy. We all have sinned. Apologizing (saying you are sorry) naturally follows, as does asking for forgiveness. **Making amends, however, is impossible.** This is where you accept His mercy and His Son, for when you accept His Son, you accept His forgiveness.

At this point, when you ask God for forgiveness, He forgives you (John 1:9). God can forgive you because you have accepted His mercy and His Son. But, as usual, a lot of people have a hard time actually receiving forgiveness. Again, I have to ask, ***what's the point in asking for forgiveness if you aren't going to receive it?***

Free to Enjoy: Life without condemnation

When you actually receive God's forgiveness, you are forever freed from a life of condemnation. Tragically, a lot of Christians live in a perpetual stage of negativity, confusion, and depression. They sin and then try to do whatever it takes to make themselves "feel" forgiven. But the truth is, the price has been paid for all sin (past, present, and future) and forgiveness (for past, present, and future sin) has been given to us.

> *"Thankfully, there is no sin that humanity is capable of committing that is behond God's reach to firgive."*
> – *Dr. Sawak Sarju*

Yes, when we sin we should confess it to God, but this does not mean we should wallow in condemnation. In confessing our sin to God, we are agreeing with Him that what we did was wrong. At this point, as Charles Stanley points out, "We may grieve the heart of God, but it doesn't break His fellowship with us."

When we confess our sin, God releases us from condemnation, just as Romans 8:1 says, "*There is therefore now no condemnation for those who are in Christ Jesus.*" His love toward us has not changed one bit! What's more, He was not condemning us in the first place!

After you confess, thank God for His forgiveness.

Free to Enjoy: God's acceptance

The more you understand what God has done to forgive you, the more it opens your eyes to see just how much He loves you! Nagging thoughts about being unworthy, about your sin being too "bad" to be forgiven, or about God not caring for you ***can forever be put to rest!*** He paid too great of a price.

Once and for all, receive His acceptance!

Know also that when God accepts you, you are forever accepted! There is nothing you can do to make Him accept you more or accept you less.

With that truth in your heart, let your confidence soar! That is why those who receive God's forgiveness should be the most joyful, confident, peaceful, loving, and forgiving people on the planet!

Free to Enjoy: Your full potential

It is my passion to help people reach their full potential. That is why I started the companies I started and why I do what I do. That is why I've written and produced hundreds of programs, books, booklets, CDs, and DVDs. All of it is designed to help you reach your full potential.

But the honest truth is that you can study every book, work through every program, listen to every recording, and watch every video, and still not reach your full potential if you don't have a personal relationship with Jesus Christ. He is what makes it all possible.

Just like it is always our individual choice to forgive, so it is our individual choice to accept His offer.

Free to Enjoy: Countless other benefits

Forgiveness comes with more benefits than could be written here. Here is a short list of what you are able to enjoy as a result of forgiveness:

- Peace
- Joy
- Freedom
- Health
- Strength
- Self-control

- Power
- Gratefulness
- Restoration
- Growth
- Passion
- Money
- A clean conscience
- Increased opportunity
- Hope
- Creativity
- Energy
- Sleep
- Advancement
- Time together with family
- Contentment
- Communication with loved ones
- A better relationship with God
- A brighter future

Forgiveness has an uncanny way of bringing incredible good out of incredibly bad situations. It's amazing, nothing less than a miracle.

Whatever your situation, let forgiveness set you free.

Putting forgiveness to work in my own life

Several years ago, I entered into a real estate deal with 15 other partners. These partners were fellow Christians and I thought that this was going to be a long-term, mutually beneficial friendship. Things went bad very quickly and every single partner walked away ... leaving me holding the bag.

I've paid close to $40,000 a month for almost seven years because they all backed out. I chose to forgive them, but interestingly, not one of them has apologized, much less made restitution.

Forgiving and showing mercy sometimes comes with a big price tag, but it's worth any price to be free!

Making Forgiveness a Habit

Make it second nature!

Forgiveness is a choice, but you want the choice to become second nature to you. The faster you choose to forgive, the quicker you can enjoy the benefits. In short, forgiveness must become a habit.

The habit of forgiveness begins where every habit begins: ***in your mind.*** What you ponder and think about will lead to what you say and do. After all, isn't forgiveness a choice before it is an action? That is because once you choose to forgive, it is just a matter of time before you do!

Granted, it might not be easy—*it will probably be very difficult*—but if you want forgiveness to set you free, it will!

Over and over, sometimes on a minute-by-minute basis, choose to forgive. Make it part of your vocabulary. Make it part of your mindset. And finally, as a result, it will be part of your life! It takes time to develop an I-will-forgive-you-regardless-of-what-you-do-to-me mentality, but when you truly want to forgive, you will!

> *The faster you choose to forgive, the quicker you can enjoy the benefits.*

Thoughts and actions lead to habits like this:

Sow a thought, reap an action,
Sow an action, reap a habit.

That is how you create a habit—any habit—that you want in your life. And once you have a habit in place, it works like this:

> **Sow a habit, reap character,**
> **Sow character, reap a destiny.**

It is your choice, and by the looks of things, you have chosen well. I commend you! The habit of forgiveness begins by you choosing to forgive.

Now that you are free, what will you do?

Applying Forgiveness

Forgiveness only works when applied. For that reason, the following ACTION STEPS were designed to help you do just that.

Action Step #1

Read the Book

The reason that *Forgiveness ... The Ultimate Miracle* was not written from a research point of view, an academic point of view, or a theological point of view was so that you would have a chance to read, hear, and even taste real forgiveness.

This is real, 100% practical forgiveness. This is what it's all about. In addition to the true stories from counselors, friends, pastors, employees, and acquaintances, I included plenty of my own stories. You no doubt have many of your own stories of forgiveness.

Become a master at forgiveness. Apply and re-apply these principles and steps to forgiveness as often as you need. Read and re-read chapters as often as you need. Don't rush. Allow what you read to set you free. Your freedom is worth it!

Action Step #2

Use the "Practical Application Guide"

Access your FREE **Practical Application Guide** to *Forgiveness ... The Ultimate Miracle* by going www.pauljmeyer.com. Forgiveness should be practical, and the **Practical Application Guide** has been specifically designed to challenge you, encourage you, and motivate you to forgive. It is powerful!

It will cause you to dig deeper and to think harder about forgiveness than you might have ever done before. Are you ready to be practical ... and take your forgiveness to the next level?

Your FREE **Practical Application Guide** is available right now at www.pauljmeyer.com.

Action Step #3

Experience 12-Weeks of "Forgiveness Training"

Because 62% of new ideas are never accepted until we have heard them six times, spaced repetition is the perfect tool to overcome the stubbornness of unforgiveness.

Over the years, I have sent weekly writings on forgiveness to different people all over the world. What I've found is amazing! Even the hardest of hearts melted! That is the power of spaced repetition.

Because the results have been tremendous, I have created a 12-week "Forgiveness Training" that you can use for yourself or give to someone else. And the price? FREE!

Go to www.pauljmeyer.com, click on the "**Forgiveness Training**" link, and enjoy the training. It will be emailed to you twice a week for 12 weeks.

Remember, 62% of new ideas get into your head—*and then into your heart*—only after you've heard them six times. Use repetition to break any wall of unforgiveness.

Action Step #4

Study other Paul J. Meyer books, booklets, CDs, DVDs, and online trainings

Paul J. Meyer has much to say about success in every area of your life and is considered by many to be the founder of the personal development industry.

A millionaire at age 27, Paul launched his dream business: Success Motivation® Institute, Inc. (SMI), dedicated to motivating people to their full potential.© The product line has expanded to include full-length courses and programs in personal achievement and leadership development. Combined sales of programs written by Meyer exceed two billion dollars worldwide, more than any other author in this field.

The Meyer family also owns and operates over 40 companies around the world, and the Paul and Jane Meyer Family Foundation supports more than 30 charities and ministries worldwide. Although Meyer claims he officially retired at age 70, he maintains his lifetime goal of "doing all the good he can, for as many people as he can, in as many ways as he can, for as long as he can." As a result, his vision and activity of the future have only increased.

At www.pauljmeyer.com, you will find many of his life-changing books, booklets, CDs, DVDs, and online trainings.

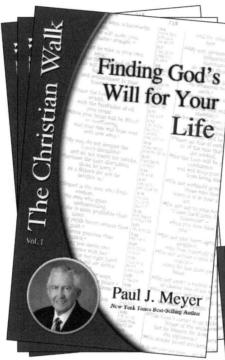

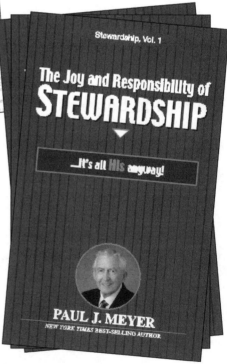